GameMaker Fundamentals

Learn GML Programming to Start Making Amazing Games

Ben Tyers

Apress®

GameMaker Fundamentals: Learn GML Programming to Start Making Amazing Games

Ben Tyers
Worthing, West Sussex, UK

ISBN-13 (pbk): 978-1-4842-8712-5
https://doi.org/10.1007/978-1-4842-8713-2

ISBN-13 (electronic): 978-1-4842-8713-2

Managing Director, Apress Media LLC: Welmoed Spahr
Acquisitions Editor: Spandana Chatterjee
Development Editor: Spandana Chatterjee
Coordinating Editor: Mark Powers

Cover designed by eStudioCalamar

Cover image by Freepik (www.freepik.com)

Distributed to the book trade worldwide by Apress Media, LLC, 1 New York Plaza, New York, NY 10004, U.S.A. Phone 1-800-SPRINGER, fax (201) 348-4505, e-mail orders-ny@springer-sbm.com, or visit www. springeronline.com. Apress Media, LLC is a California LLC and the sole member (owner) is Springer Science + Business Media Finance Inc (SSBM Finance Inc). SSBM Finance Inc is a **Delaware** corporation.

For information on translations, please e-mail booktranslations@springernature.com; for reprint, paperback, or audio rights, please e-mail bookpermissions@springernature.com.

Apress titles may be purchased in bulk for academic, corporate, or promotional use. eBook versions and licenses are also available for most titles. For more information, reference our Print and eBook Bulk Sales web page at http://www.apress.com/bulk-sales.

Any source code or other supplementary material referenced by the author in this book is available to readers on GitHub (https://github.com/Apress). For more detailed information, please visit http://www. apress.com/source-code.

Printed on acid-free paper

Table of Contents

TABLE OF CONTENTS

About the Author

Ben Tyers is an expert GameMaker user, developer, coder, and trainer, with over 10 years of experience in GameMaker. He has authored several books on GameMaker for game application developers. He runs a popular gaming website, which features accessible games that can be played by gamers with physical disabilities, with around one new game added every month. He has learnt GML coding to a reasonable level and has picked up many skills, tips and tricks, and methodology for making games in GameMaker.

About the Technical Reviewer

 **Mark Alexander** has been a technical writer for the last 12 years, starting his career working for YoYo Games in Scotland, where he was in charge of the GameMaker documentation for almost ten years. After that, he moved on to work at Asobo Studio in France, where he is doing the technical documentation for the Microsoft Flight Simulator SDK.

In his spare time – apart from reading sci-fi, collecting Lego, and playing video games – he creates and publishes small indie games and also creates assets for people to use in GameMaker. Any time he has left after that, he dedicates to the administration of the GameMaker Community Forum.

Acknowledgments

Various Audio and Graphics Used in Game and Challenges: Permission Given to Use by Yoyogames.com. Please Do Not Redistribute These Assets.

Graphics:

Aeroplane: Pzuj/Opengameart.org – CC0

Animated Boy Sprites: Bevouliin.com/Opengameart.org – CC0

Arrow: oglsdl/Opengameart.org – CC0

Asteroids: Jasper/Opengameart.org – CC0

Bag: Flowly/Opengameart.org – CC0

Ball: Gothicfan95/Freepik.com

Barrel: Manenwolf/Opengameart.org – CC0

Beach Scene: Tgfcoder/Opengameart.org – CC0

Bee: Carriejanesart/Opengameart.org – CC0

Birds: Bevouliin.com/Opengameart.org – CC0 && CC-BY 4.0

Blue Character: Kenny/Opengameart.org – CC0

Boats: Kutejnikov/Opengameart.org – CC0

Bomb Sprite: Znevs/Opengameart.org – CC0

Boss Missile: Bevouliin.com/Opengameart.org – CC0

Boss Plane: Bevouliin.com/Opengameart.org – CC0

Bullets Set: Bevouliin.com/Opengameart.org – CC-BY 3.0

Buttons: Game Developer Studio/Opengameart.org – CC-BY 3.0

Crosshair: hc/Opengameart.org – CC0

Caveman: Hapiel/Opengameart.org – CC0

Cloud: Bananaowl/Opengameart.org – CC-BY 3.0

Clouds: Bevouliin.com/Opengameart.org – CC0

Crate: Rfc1394/Opengameart.org – CC0

Crocodile Character: Bevouliin.com/Opengameart.org – CC0

Dinosaur: Pzuj/Opengameart.org – CC0

Donuts: Game Developer Studio/Opengameart.org – CC-BY 3.0

Eggs: Ogreofwart/Opengameart.org – CC0

Elements: Game Developer Studio/Opengameart.org – CC-BY 3.0

ACKNOWLEDGMENTS

Explosion: Stumpystrust/Opengameart.org – CC0

Extra Character Sprites: Bevouliin.com/Opengameart.org – CC0

Firenall: Cethiel/Opengameart.org – CC0

Firework: Jellyfish/Opengameart.org – CC0

Fuel Collectable: Freestockimages/Opengameart.org – CC0

Fuel Gauge: JM.Atencia/Opengameart.org – CC-BY 3.0

Fish: Sylly/Opengameart.org – CC0

Forest: Ansimuz/Opengameart.org – CC0

Gems: Wenrexa/Opengameart.org – CC0

Grass Sky Backgrounds Images: Segel/Opengameart.org – CC0

Green Horn Zombie Sprites: Bevouliin.com/Opengameart.org – CC0

Green Zombie: Segel/Opengameart.org – CC0

Guns & Bullets Images: Kay Lousberg/Opengameart.org – CC0

Heart/Lives Sprite: Cdgramos/Opengameart.org – CC0

Missile Enemy: Bevouliin.com/Opengameart.org – CC0

Laser: Rawdanitsu/Opengameart.org – CC0

Missile: JM.Atencia/Opengameart.org – CC-BY 3.0

Mountain Background Images: Ansimuz/Opengameart.org – CC0

Mountain Images: Ansimuz/Opengameart.org – CC0

Mouse Icons: Qubodup/Opengameart.org – CC0

Padlocks: Rawpixel.com/Freepik.com

Plane Game Background: Bevouliin.com/Opengameart.org – CC0 && OGA-BY-3.0

Rocks: Bevouliin.com/Opengameart.org – CC0

Rotating Coin Sprites: Puddin/Opengameart.org – CC0

Rpg Character: Curt/Opengameart.org – CC-BY 3.0

Sea Background: Donte/Opengameart.org – CC0

Shinny Coins: Bevouliin.com/Opengameart.org – CC0 && CC-BY 4.0

Space Background: Satur9/Opengameart.org – CC0

Space Parallax Images: Ansimuz/Opengameart.org – CC0

Spaceship: Bevouliin.com/Opengameart.org – CC-BY 3.0 & CC0

Spiky Land Monster: Bevouliin.com/Opengameart.org – CC0

Star: Jellyfish/Opengameart.org – CC0

Tileset: Buch/Opengameart.org – CC0

Top Down Zombie Images: Riley Gombart/Opengameart.org – CC0

Underwater: Game Developer Studio/Opengameart.org – CC-BY 3.0

Walking Green Monster Sprites: Bevouliin.com/Opengameart.org – CC0

Wall: Beaterator/Opengameart.org – CC0

Audio:

Beep: Thisusernameis/Freesound.org – CC0

Bird Sound: JackWilDesign/Freesound.org – CC0

Bell Sound: Se2001/Freesound.org – CC0

Coins (long) dj997/Freesound.org – CC-BY 3.0

Dance Music: Davejf/Freesound.org – CC0

Explosion Sound: Derplayer/Freesound.org – CC0

Firework: Rudmer_rotteveel/Freesound.org – CC0

Gun Sound: Mrrap4food/Freesound.org – CC0

Heavy Beet Music: Jpmusic82/Freesound.org – CC0

Machine Gun Sound: Pgi/Freesound.org – CC0

Melody Music: Drfx/Freesound.org – CC0

Menu Sound: Apenguin73/Freesound.org – CC0

Nuke Sound: Tristanluigi/Freesound.org – CC0

Ouch: Legnalegna55/Freesound.org – CC0

Ping Sound: Wilhellboy/Freesound.org – CC0

Plane Game Level Music: Rezoner/Opengameart.org – CC-BY 3.0

Plane Game Menu Music: Cynicmusic/Opengameart.org – CC0

Plane Game Sound Effects: Subspaceaudio/Opengameart.org – CC0

Random Sound 1: Mosrod/Freesound.org – CC0

Random Sound 2: Littlerainyseasons/Freesound.org – CC0

Random Sound 3: Elfstonepress/Freesound.org – CC0

Random Sound 4: Alanmcki/Freesound.org – CC0

Random Sound 5: Jeremysykes/Freesound.org – CC0

Rocket Sound: Derplayer/Freesound.org – CC0

Introduction

A note from the author:

Congratulations!

You are about to learn the basics of GameMaker and potentiallystart a career in game making.

This book is an introduction to the game-making process, an introduction to GameMaker, and other considerations when making your first game.

GameMaker is a powerful piece of software for making games. This book only covers the basics but is a great place to start. This book uses the updated 2022 edition.

Best of luck with your game-making endeavors.

Ben

Welcome

The purpose of this book is to provide you with some of the knowledge that I have acquired. I make no claim that I'm the best coder or designer, but I do have a proficient understanding that I would like to instill in other budding game makers.

The book is broken down into 29 main chapters and three appendixes: one that pulls together the knowledge you gained from the book to create a game, one offering programming challenges, and one covering how to get set up with GameMaker and its IDE.

The main chapters each introduce a separate programming concept and explain what it is used for and how it is applied, along with some examples. Each of these chapters then finishes with some assignments.

The game chapter details how to make a simple shooting game.

You are then presented with 65 programming challenges, each of which adds a new feature to the game you have just made.

Source Code

All source code in this book can be downloaded from `github.com/apress/` `gamemaker-fundamentals.`

CHAPTER 1

Variables

When using GameMaker, there are two main types of variables that you will use often. They are strings and numbers (reals and integers). You can do many different things with variables. They can be used for performing calculations and drawing information on the screen. You will use variables for such things as

- Keeping track of score, health, and lives

- Drawing the values of score, health and lives

- Processing data and performing actions based on their values

- Using values in calculations

- Making an object move

- Displaying values, as text or graphically

- Saving the player's progress

- Setting the difficulty of a game or level

- Sending values for online highscores

- Setting initial positions of objects and how they move

- Checking for a weapon's availability or power

- Drawing text to explain what a player must do

- And many more

Note   There are several variable types such as instance, local, and global. You will focus mainly on instance and global variables.

© Ben Tyers 2023
B. Tyers, *GameMaker Fundamentals*, https://doi.org/10.1007/978-1-4842-8713-2_1

Some variables automatically have global scope, such as health, lives, and score.

Note   It should be noted that these preceding three variables may be deprecated in the future, so you'll need to create your own variables with global scope if you wish them to be accessible game wide, for example, global.my_score.

Global variables have scope across the whole game and can be accessed, read, and changed from anywhere else within your game. For example:

```
global.target=100;
```

Generally you would set your global values at the very start of the game, for example, some code that is run on your game splash screen:

```
/// @description Set up global values
lives=6;
score=0;
health=100;
global.target=100;
global.enemies_to_kill=20;
room_goto(room_menu);
```

Note   Failure to declare any global value prior to using it will result in an error and crash your game. As such, these are generally set at the start of the game, usually in splash screen room; this is explained later in this book.

If you want to make another variable global in scope, you can put global in front of the variable, for example, global.level.

Instance variables, for example, x and y, and hp, are generally accessible for the object that set them. (Actually, you can access and change instance variables from other objects, but we won't go into that just now.)

Local variables have the scope of the code block that is using them, for example:

```
var size=5;
```

A basic example usage would be the following:

```
for (var loop = 0; loop< 20; loop++)
{
    draw_text(20+(loop*25,30,loop);
}
```

which would draw the numbers 0 through 19.

An advanced example may look something like this:

```
/// @description Shooting bullet control
if can_shoot_bullet
{
    var bullet=instance_create_layer( x,y,"bullets",obj_player_bullet);
    //spawn the bullet
    bullet.speed=4;//set the speed of bullet
    bullet.direction=image_angle;//match direction to that of the plane
    bullet.image_angle=image_angle;//make the bullet point to direction of
                                    movement
    can_shoot_bullet=false;
    alarm[0]=game_get_speed(gamespeed_fps);
    global.shots_fired++;//update shot count
    audio_play_sound(snd_player_bullet,1,false);
}
```

This would mean that the game would not remember the bullet variable once the code block is completed.

Local variables will mainly be used for data and structures that are no longer required once some data has been processed, and for variables that are outside the scope of the code block. These types of variables help prevent memory leaks.

A memory leak is, for example, when your program keeps creating new items (i.e., variables, or instances) without properly removing them, gradually eating up available memory space – which will crash your game and most likely crash the device that is running it.

The basic code for drawing text is

```
draw_text(x_position,y_position,text);
```

It's good practice to remember to set the font and formatting prior to drawing any text.

Note   Text formatting (font, colors, alignment) will be continued for any future drawing of text until you tell the program otherwise, so get into the habit of setting it before drawing anything.

You can create a font, as shown in Figure 1-1.

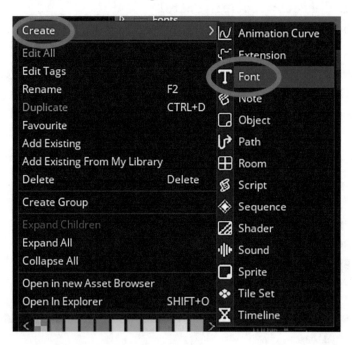

Figure 1-1. *Creating a font asset*

First, let's set up a font to use for this chapter, as shown in Figure 1-2.

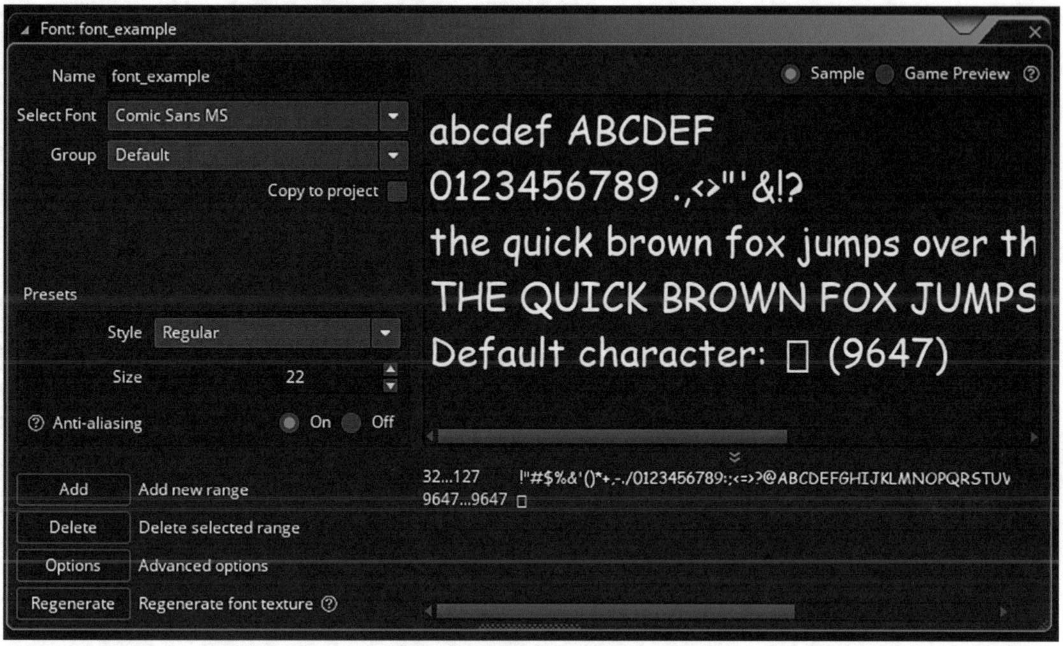

Figure 1-2. *Setting a font to be used for this chapter*

A real working example would be: To draw text "Hello World" at position 100x100. Create an object, **obj_example**, with the following code placed in the **Draw Event**, as shown in Figure 1-3.

```
/// @description Draw example text
draw_set_font(font_example);
draw_text(100,100,"Hello World");
```

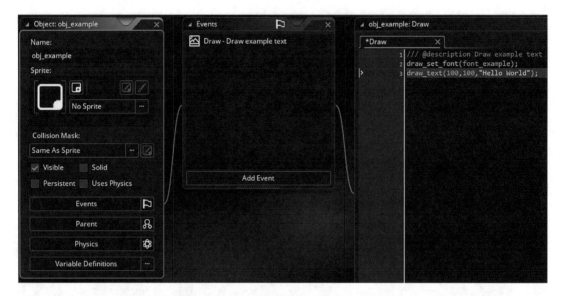

Figure 1-3. *Draw event code*

Drag an instance of this object into the room onto the **Instances** layer and click the run button, as shown in Figure 1-4.

Figure 1-4. *Showing where to click*

You'll then see the text drawn onscreen, like that in Figure 1-5.

Figure 1-5. *Showing some example text drawn*

To draw a variable with a number (an integer), for example, add a **Create Event** and put the following code:

```
/// @description Set up a value
value=20;
```

And in the **Draw Event**, put the following code:

```
/// @description Draw Value
draw_set_font(font_example);
draw_text(200,200,value);
```

Test the game and check the expected value is drawn.

Next, we'll combine some variables, so change the **Create Event** to

```
/// @description Set up values
text="My Name Is Ben";
age=36;
```

Set **Draw Event** to combine these values, noting that you change the value of age to a string so they can be combined without error:

```
/// @description Draw example text
draw_set_font(font_example);
draw_text(100,100,text+" My age is "+string(age));
```

If you are drawing just text or a numerical variable as a separate statement, then the preceding is not required, so, for example, the following would work fine:

```
line="Hello World";
draw_text(30,30,line);
value=4500;
draw_text(30,60,value);
```

When run, you'll see the following on your screen, as shown in Figure 1-6.

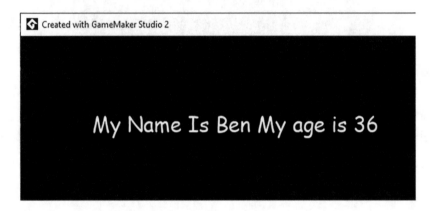

Figure 1-6. *Drawing text and variables combined*

Numbers can be an integer, such as 5, or a real which includes decimals, such as 11.8. Double-click on **obj_example** in the resource tree. Change the **Create Event** code to

```
my_age=43;
```

You can of course add strings together (called concatenation), for example:

```
first_name="Ben";
last_name="Tyers";
my_name=first_name+" "+last_name;
```

You can do mathematical operations on numbers and then draw the result, for example, the following where if you were to draw the value of total_cost on the screen it would show as 45:

```
cakes=9;
cost=5;
total_cost=cakes*cost;
```

GameMaker allows lots of math operations to be performed on numbers. For example:

```
a=30;
b=8;
```

So, the following:

```
c=a mod b;
```

would set c as 6 (b goes into a three times with a remainder of 6).

```
c=a div b;
```

would set c as 3 (b goes into a three times).

```
c=a / b;
```

would set c with a value of 3.75 (approx.).

You can generate random numbers using several functions:

```
number=irandom(100);
```

The preceding would set a random whole number between 0 and 100 inclusive. For example, if you made the **Create Event** code:

```
number=irandom(100);
```

set the **Draw Event** to

```
/// @description Draw example text
draw_set_font(font_example);
draw_text(100,100,number);
```

and add the following to a **Step Event**:

```
/// @description Restart room
if keyboard_check_pressed (vk_space) room_restart();
```

If you test this, each time you press space a new random number will be set.
Numbers can also be real (generally not whole numbers like integers), for example: 17.284 (which may contain more decimals).

Note   Each time you run a game that uses random numbers, the same sequence will be generated which makes testing easier. This does not necessarily apply to compiled games. You can override this by calling `randomize()` once upon game starting (within your first object).

Equally, you can change a string to a value; however, this should only be used if you are sure the string only contains numbers, as text will throw an error. An example of this would be as follows:

The **Create Event**:

```
/// @description Set up values
a="3.46";
b=real(a);
```

and a **Draw Event**:

```
/// @description Draw example text
draw_set_font(font_example);
draw_text(100,100,b);
```

If you wish to get just the numerical values from a string, the function `string_digits` can be used, for example, a **Create Event** with

```
/// @description Remove numbers from a string
sentence="Ben is 34 years old";
value=string_digits(sentence);
```

and a **Draw Event** with

```
/// @description Draw value
draw_set_font(font_example);
draw_text(100,100,value);
```

which would draw the following as shown in Figure 1-7.

Figure 1-7. *Showing numerical values taken from a string*

Note   The following should really only be used for testing purposes; for an actual game, look into using get_integer_async and get_string_async.

Extra Useful Code:

```
number=get_integer("Enter a Number",0);
city=get_string("City","Enter Where You Were Born");
```

You can also set the color of drawing text, for example:

```
/// @description Draw some formatted text
draw_set_font(font_example);
draw_set_colour(c_yellow);
draw_text(100,100,"This is some example text");
```

which would draw the example text in color yellow. There are other built in colors, as shown in Figure 1-8.

Colour	Appearance	RGB Value	Colour	Appearance	RGB Value
c_aqua		0,255,255	c_olive		128,128,0
c_black		0,0,0	c_orange		255,160,64
c_blue		0,0,255	c_purple		128,0,128
c_dkgray		64,64,64	c_red		255,0,0
c_fuchsia		255,0,255	c_silver		192,192,192
c_gray		128,128,128	c_teal		0,128,128
c_green		0,128,0	c_white		255,255,255
c_lime		0,255,0	c_yellow		255,255,0
c_ltgray		192,192,192	c_olive		128,128,0
c_maroon		128,0,0	c_orange		255,160,64
c_navy		0,0,128	c_purple		128,0,128

Figure 1-8. *Showing color constants*

You can also define your own custom colors; this is explained in Chapter 3.

You can also set horizontal and vertical alignment.

For horizontal, you can use

```
draw_set_halign(fa_left);
draw_set_halign(fa_right);
draw_set_halign(fa_center);
```

and for vertical you can use

```
draw_set_valign(fa_top);
draw_set_valign(fa_bottom);
draw_set_valign(fa_middle);
```

Some example code could look like this:

```
/// @description Draw some formatted text
draw_set_font(font_example);
draw_set_colour(c_yellow);
draw_set_halign(fa_left);
draw_text(500,130,"This is some example text");
draw_set_colour(c_white);
draw_set_halign(fa_right);
draw_text(500,160,"This is some more example text");
draw_set_colour(c_green);
draw_set_halign(fa_center);
draw_text(500,190,"This is yet another example");
```

which would look like Figure 1-9 when run.

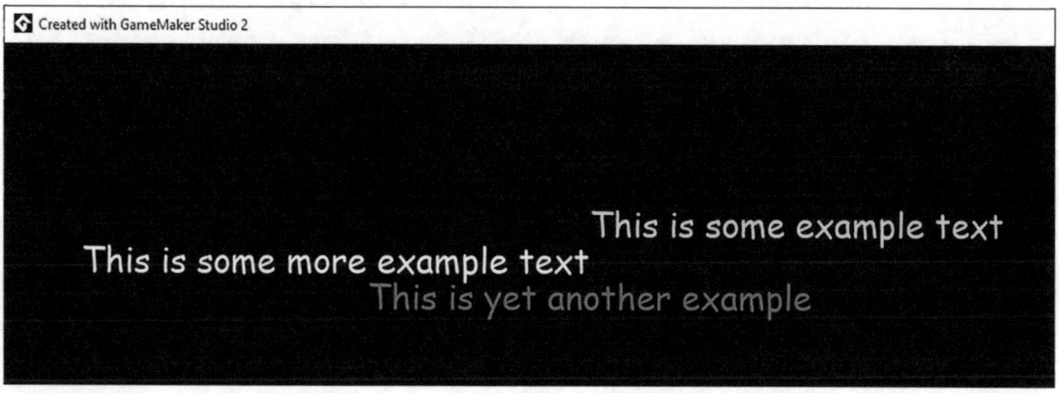

Figure 1-9. *Showing some examples of text formatting*

You've probably realized by now the first two values in draw_text relate to the position where something is drawn, this not only applies to text but also for things you'll do in game such as drawing a sprite or creating an effect.

The top-left position in a room is 0,0. When you have an open room, you can see the coordinates of the mouse in the lower left corner as shown in Figure 1-10.

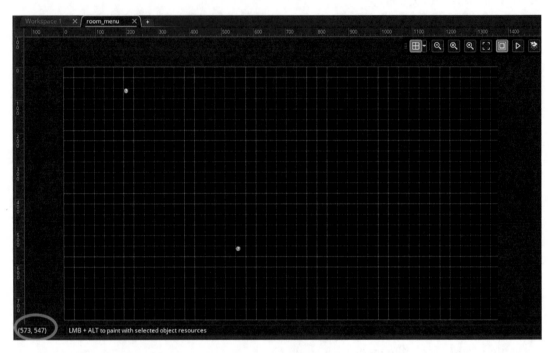

Figure 1-10. *Showing room coordinates*

You should now understand the difference between strings and reals, how to use them and what they can be used for, and how to draw and set some basic formatting.

Basic Assignments

A) Allow the user to enter their name, age, and date of birth. Draw these values on screen using font, color, and alignment.

B) Make a program that takes in five numbers and calculates the average; draw the numbers on screen, along with the average.

Advance Assignments

C) Allow user to enter a day of the month, add the correct ordinal indicator, that is, st (1st), rd (3rd), nd(52nd).

D) Allow a user to enter their date of birth (day, month, and year). Draw on screen the day of the week they were born on.

Useful Functions

```
variable=irandom_range(100,200);
```

would set a random whole integer between 100 and 200 inclusive.

```
starting= -97;
variable=abs(starting);
```

would set variable as 97. This code changes a negative value into a positive one, and keeps a positive value positive.

```
variable=sign(-28);
```

would set variable as -1, a positive number would return as 1.

You can increment a variable by 1 using any of the following:

```
value++;
value+=1;
value=value+1;
```

Sometimes you may want to a keep a value between ranges; here is one (of many) method:

```
x= clamp(x, 0, room_width);
```

which keeps x between 0 and the room width.

Summary

After completing this first chapter, you should be aware of the main variable types that you will use when you create a game.

You should also understand some basic math operations that can be performed upon variables.

You should now know about drawing text at certain room positions, and the importance of formatting drawn text just prior to the use of drawing functions.

You should also know that any fonts needed to be drawn within the game require being set up.

The rest of the book will assume that you have learnt all of the preceding, so I suggest you take a moment to re-read this chapter and make sure you didn't miss anything.

CHAPTER 2

Conditionals

Conditional statements are used to compare or evaluate expressions and perform actions based on whether they evaluate as **true** or **false**.

You will use conditionals a lot in your game to make things happen (or not happen). For example:

- Making an instance change direction upon collision with another instance
- Basic AI for enemies such as shooting a projectile or moving
- Play a sound effect in response to something happening
- A level unlock system based on the player's score or when they collect
- something
- Fire a projectile or move in response to a mouse click or keypress
- Using the middle mouse button to change a weapon
- Allow an upgrade if a player has enough cash
- Determine the player's current movement state
- Make graphical effects happen
- Determining if a weapon is available or not

Conditionals evaluate a mathematical expression, and will perform code depending on whether it evaluates as true or false:

```
a=1;
b=2;
c=3;
```

© Ben Tyers 2023
B. Tyers, *GameMaker Fundamentals*, https://doi.org/10.1007/978-1-4842-8713-2_2

Would give the following results:

```
if (a+b)==c returns true.
if a==b returns false.
```

Note   Use == when evaluating conditionals, as opposed to a single =. Although GameMaker may accept a single =, this is bad practice as it may be redcated in future versions, additionally most other programming languages use a double ==, so best to avoid habits now that may break your game in the future. It also makes scanning large blocks of code easier, when debugging your games.ctual, code will look like this:

```
if a+b==c
{
    //do something if true
    show_debug_message("This Is True");
}
else
{
    // do something if false
    show_debug_message("This Is False");
}
```

So, the preceding example would evaluate as true and display the message "This Is True" in the console output, as shown in Figure 2-1.

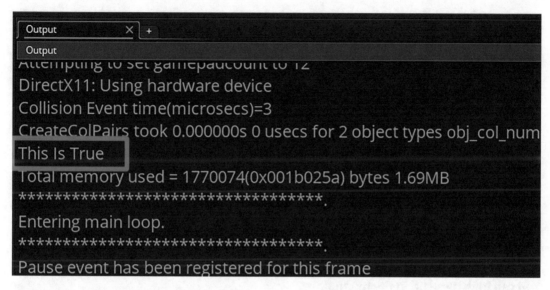

Figure 2-1. *Showing console output*

Note the use of the curly brackets { and }any code within these will be executed, depending on whether the code evaluates as true or false.

You can add ! before an expression. This will negate it, making a true into a false and vice versa. For example, the following will execute if a does not equal b, which it doesn't, so the message will be shown:

```
if !a==b
{
    //do something if true
    show_message("This Is True");
}
```

You can test if a sound is playing or not:

```
if audio_is_playing(snd_level_1_music)
{
    //do something, for example stop the music
}
```

You can test the pressing of a mouse button (which will be executed once when the button is pressed):

```
if mouse_check_button_pressed(mb_left)
```

```
{
     //This block will execute
}
```

You can also check for keyboard presses, for example, the following (which will execute for each frame of the game whilst the key is held down):

```
if keyboard_check(ord("Z"))
{
     //This block will execute
}
```

ord is a function which allows for identification of keyboard input within your game. There are also key codes identified with vk_ which are used for non-alphanumeric keys. You can look these up in the manual.

Variables can also have a value of true or false:

```
weapon=true;
power_up=false;
```

For example, you could do the following, which would not execute as the value of this variable is currently set to false:

```
if power_up
{
     //Add some code to increase weapon strength
}
```

The following code would execute the code in the first block:

```
if weapon
{
     //This block would execute
}
else
{
     //This block would not execute
}
```

You can also use operands and mathematical comparisons when checking a conditional:

```
a=1;
b=2;
c=4;
d=4;
```

    if a<b returns as true.

    if b>c returns as false.

You can also evaluate using <= to check if a value is less than or equal to:

```
if c<=d
{
    //This block would execute
}
```

You can also use and >= to check and determine if a value is greater than or equal to something.

Logical operators can also be used, for example && and and, || and or.

An example which would check for the keypress of W or up arrow:

```
if keyboard_check(ord("W")) or keyboard_check(vk_up)
{
    //This block will run if W or up arrow pressed
}
```

You can check for two simultaneous keypresses:

```
if keyboard_check(ord("Z")) and keyboard_check(vk_left)
{
    //This block will execute if Z and the left arrow is pressed
}
```

Basic Assignments

A) Set a variable string as a password. Allow user to enter a guess. Display whether the correct password has been entered.

B)   Allow user to enter their name, display each character (and previous letters) as the player types.

Project Note: Look up usage of `keyboard_string`

Advance Assignment

C)   Display an instance on screen for one second. Player to then click where the instance was displayed. Display the distance in pixels for how close the mouse click was. Allow keypress of R to restart the game.

Useful Functions

You can get a room name, and make something happen, for example:

```
name=room_get_name(room);
if name=="level_2"
{
    //spawn 2 enemies
}
```

You could check how many of an instance are present and do something like:

```
if instance_number(obj_enemy)<=5 && message=false
{
   message=true;
        audio_play_sound(snd_5_enemies_left,0,false);
}
```

Summary

After working through this chapter, you should have a strong basic knowledge of conditionals. You can now compare values, detect mouse buttons and keypresses.

Conditionals will be used a lot within this book (and your game). Refer back to this chapter if you need to.

CHAPTER 3

Drawing Shapes

GameMaker is very flexible when it comes to drawing. There are several built-in functions for drawing basic and advanced geometric shapes. Drawing is done by positioning sprites or vertices within the room. In GameMaker, x relates to how many pixels across the screen and y for how many down. The position at the top left is 0,0. This chapter will introduce you to the basics of drawing.

Basic geometric shapes can be used for such things as

- Drawing the border of a room.

- Making popup text boxes.

- Creating effects when changing rooms.

- Making various graphical effects.

- Drawing grids, for example for inventory.

Note YoYo games is a British company, spelling is in British English, though American spelling can be used, for example colour or color. For example: `draw_set_colour(c_red)` or `draw_set_color(c_blue)`, you can set your preferred spelling in the Preferences. Drawing code must always be placed within a **Draw Event**. There are several options available for drawing, but for now we'll just focus on the Draw Event. Figure 3-1 shows how to select this event.

© Ben Tyers 2023
B. Tyers, *GameMaker Fundamentals*, https://doi.org/10.1007/978-1-4842-8713-2_3

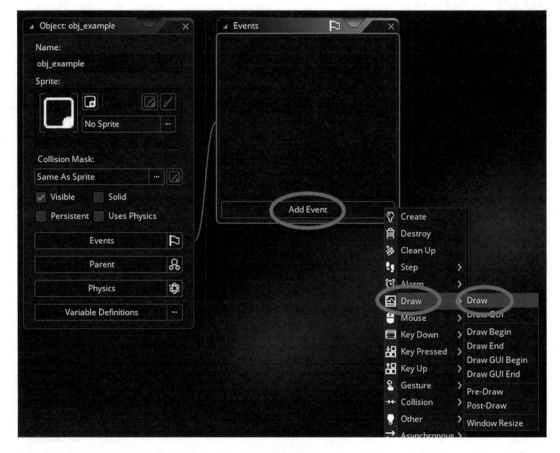

Figure 3-1. *Showing how to select draw event*

There are several built-in color constants that can be used, see Figure 1-9 back in Chapter 1.

The following code can be used to set a drawing color:

```
draw_set_colour(c_blue);
```

Colors can also be set using their hexadecimal values prefixed with a '$' character, which in the format used in GameMaker is in BBGGRR, for example:

```
draw_set_colour($00ff00);
```

You can also set the color using the more known RGB color system. The function for this is make_colour_rgb, an example being:

```
var my_colour=make_colour_rgb(15,90,255);
```

```
draw_set_colour(my_colour);
draw_circle(100,100,80,true);
```

which would draw the outline of a circle in the defined color. Setting the value true to false would draw a solid circle.

Note   You can set up global values at game start, so your defined colors are accessible by all objects in your game. Very useful if you will be using a lot of custom color in your game. For example: `global.colour_mix_1=make_colour_rgb(80,90,60);`

You can draw a single line in green between two points:

```
draw_set_colour(c_green);
draw_line(10,10,90,90);
```

The following will draw a solid yellow rectangle. Using true would draw the outline only:

```
draw_set_colour(c_yellow);
draw_rectangle(25,25,90,90,false);
```

There are many other shapes that can be drawn, again false for filled or true for outline only:

```
draw_ellipse(x1,y1,x2,y2,false); //draws a solid ellipse
draw_roundrect(x1,y1,x2,y2,true); //draw an outline of a rectangle with
rounded corners
draw_triangle(x1,y1,x2,y2,x3,y3,true); //draws an outline of a triangle
```

There are many other drawing shapes and functions. Look up the manual for functions starting with draw_ and have a play-around using them.

Note   When in the code window, you can click on a function with the middle mouse button to quickly look up its entry in the manual.

Basic Projects

A) Draw a chessboard in black and white, using appropriate drawing functions.

B) Use draw functions to draw a floor plan of the room you are in. Use different colors for chairs, tables, lockers, etc.

Advance Project

C) Using drawing functions to draw a representation of the Mona Lisa, limit yourself to 30 minutes.

It is also possible to draw a sequence of connected lines using primitives. For example:

```
draw_primitive_begin(pr_linestrip);
draw_vertex(10,10);
draw_vertex(10,90);
draw_vertex(90,120);
draw_vertex(120,180);
draw_vertex(200,200);
draw_primitive_end();
```

will draw a shape on screen.

A primitive is a collection of points that are connected to each other by lines. This has the advantage over the basic draw_line function as you only need to reference the next point to draw to (as opposed to stating the start and end point).

Useful Functions

Sometimes you may wish to set the alpha of something you are drawing. Setting an alpha changes its transparency (from 0 which is fully transparent to 1 which if fully opaque). This can apply to text, shapes, primitives and sprites, etc.

For example:

```
draw_set_alpha(0.5);
```

```
draw_set_colour(c_red);
draw_roundrect(20,20,880,200,false);
draw_set_alpha(1);//set back so other objects are not affected
```

Which would draw a red rectangle with rounded corners at 50% transparancy.
You also draw a rectangle with a gradient of two colors for example:

```
draw_roundrect_colour_ext(50,50,300,200, 5, 5, c_red, c_green, false);
```

You can also draw text with a choice of four colors, and alpha, for example:

```
draw_text_colour(200,200,"Some Example Text",c_red,c_green,c_yellow,c_
blue,1);
```

Summary

You should now be comfortable in setting colors, drawing various geometric shapes, and have better understanding of room co-ordinates.

CHAPTER 4

More Drawing

There are also lots more drawing functions for formatting text, and for drawing sprites. This chapter will introduce you to them.

Text can be used for such things:

- Scores and health

- Player names

- Game information

- Pop-up text

- Dialogue between characters

- Menu options

You will want to use sprites for such things as:

- Displaying the main player

- Drawing lives as images

- Displaying what weapons are currently available

- Various in-game buttons

- Instances the player can walk or jump on

- Enemy instances

- Game info such as health or timers

Note Ensure you only try to draw variables that have already been defined – failure to do so will cause an error and crash your game.

Create a new project in GameMaker, along with a new object **obj_example**.

© Ben Tyers 2023
B. Tyers, *GameMaker Fundamentals*, https://doi.org/10.1007/978-1-4842-8713-2_4

To use drawing functions, they need to be placed within one of the Drawing Events.

Note   Ideally, you should use drawing events for actual drawing code. Other code unrelated to drawing should be placed in an alternative event, for example, the **Step Event**.

Create a **Draw Event** for the object you just created.

Then place the following code into that event:

```
draw_text(50,50,"This is some example text");
```

This will draw the **This is some example text** at the given position.

You can also include strings and numbers, by converting the real to a string, for example:

```
var age=43;
draw_text(100,100,"I am "+string(age)+ " years old.");
```

This will draw the text **I am 43 years old**.

You can format text:

- With different colors

- Different fonts

- To have vertical and horizontal alignment

Save the code you just wrote and close the object.

Make a new font (as shown back in Chapter 1, Figure 1-1), then choose a font and size, as shown in Figure 4-1.

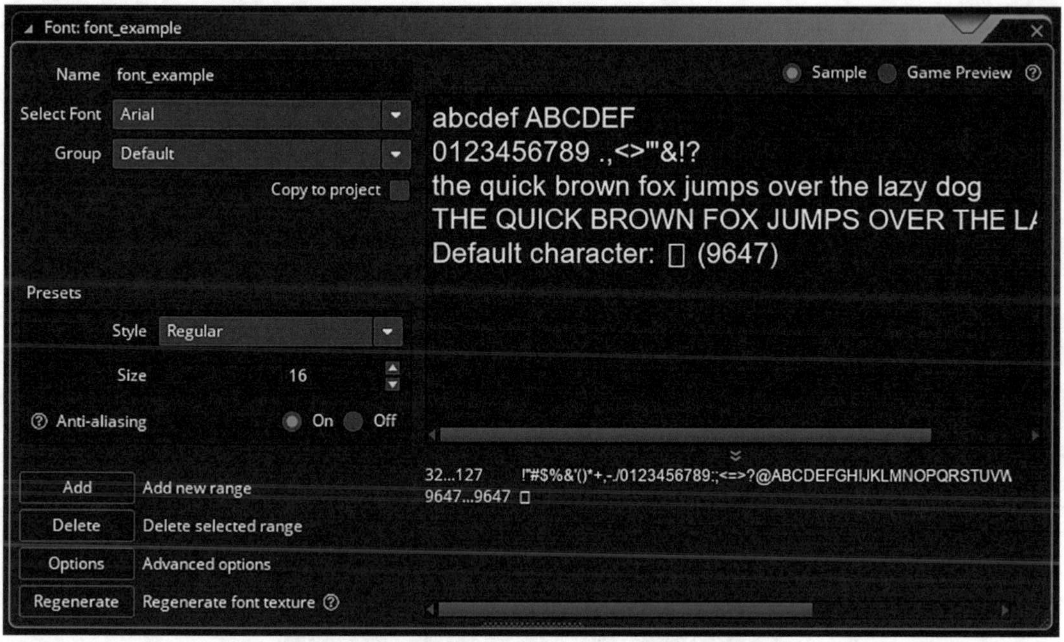

Figure 4-1. *Setting font and size*

You will now set up the drawing style using this font:

```
draw_set_font(font_example); //Set the font you just created
draw_set_colour(c_purple); //Set the colour as purple
draw_set_halign(fa_center); //Horizontal center
draw_set_valign(fa_middle); //Vertical center
draw_text(200,100,"Some Example Text");//draws text
```

Note   Formatting will remain in place for all future drawing. It is good practice to set it each time just before drawing.

The text on the previous page will be drawn centered on the horizontal and vertical, in purple and using the set font.

You can force a new line using \n

For example:

```
/// @description drawing example
draw_set_font(font_example);
```

```
var text="Hello \nWorld";
draw_text(200,200,text);
```

This would look like that shown in Figure 4-2.

Figure 4-2. *Showing force of a new line*

As mentioned previously, you can combine strings and reals. For example, you can do the following code in the **Create Event** of an object, **obj_example**:

```
/// @description An Example
name="Benjamin";
age=43;
country="England";
food="Cheese";
```

and a **Draw Event** with:

```
draw_set_font(font_example);
draw_set_halign(fa_right);
draw_set_valign(fa_top);
draw_set_colour(c_green);
draw_text(800,200,"My name is "+name+".\n I am
```

```
"+string(age)+" years old.\nI live in
"+country+".\nMy favourite food favourite food is
"+food+".");
```

Another important element of GameMaker is sprite control. You're likely to use sprites a lot in your game. The aim of this section is to draw a sprite in a few different ways. The default way of drawing the sprite with default settings would be to assign it to an object and have nothing in the **Draw Event**. You can of course use a **Draw Event** and draw the sprite manually.

Go ahead and load in a sprite from the assets folder **spiky land sprites**. Name this as **spr_test** and resize to 128x128, as shown in Figures 4-3 and 4-4.

Figure 4-3. *Showing imported and resized sprite*

You can quickly resize the image as shown in Figure 4-4.

Figure 4-4. *Showing how to resize sprite*

Go ahead and create an object **obj_example**. Put the following in the Draw Event and then test your game.

```
/// @description drawing
draw_sprite(spr_test,0,200,200);
```

This will draw the sprite **spr_test** at position 200,200. The 0 tells the program which frame of the image to draw.

You can also draw a sprite with more settings, for example:

```
draw_sprite_ext(sprite,subimage,x,y,xscale,yscale,rotation, colour,alpha);
```

This allows for more flexibility on how the sprite is drawn. Allowing you to set which sprite, subimage, scale, rotation and color blending and its alpha (transparency), it is drawn with, for example:

```
draw_sprite_ext(spr_test,0,180,120,0.8,1.5,25,c_red,1)
```

which would draw as shown in Figure 4-5.

Figure 4-5. *Example of draw_sprite_ext*

Color blending, for example, can be used to visually show damage to a player or enemy. If you want to draw a sprite with the default settings, this will be done automatically.

Sprites can also consist of multiple subimages (frames) that can be played in sequence to create an animation.

Note   GameMaker starts the subimage frame at position 0, so your first frame (if you have subimages) will be 0.

Figure 4-6 shows how to import multiple images. Click the first image, scroll the window down and click the last image while holding the Shift Key, then click on **Open**.

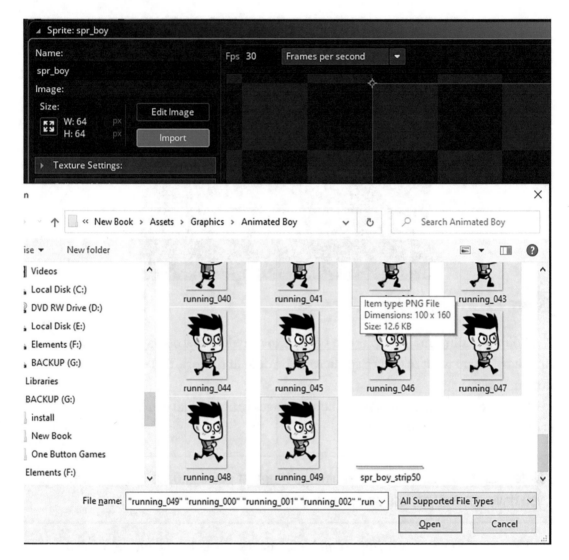

Figure 4-6. *Importing multiple images*

Assign this sprite to an object, **obj_example.**

Delete any **Draw Event** if you have one present (right click and select delete).

Note   If you are using a drawing event, you will be required to tell the program to draw the sprite. You can use draw_self() or draw_sprite_ext.()

You can also set the sprites origin, which is the position where it will be anchored when you draw it, for example, change the sprite you currently have, as shown in Figure 4-7.

Figure 4-7. *Setting the origin to middle center*

Make this change now.

Another variable that you'll find useful is image_xscale and image_yscale. This can be used to great effect in making a sprite flip when the direction changes.

Pop the following code into a new **Step Event:**

```
/// @description Movement and sprite control
if keyboard_check(vk_left)
{
    x-=2;
    image_xscale=-1;
```

```
}
if keyboard_check(vk_right)
{
    x+=2;
    image_xscale=1;
}
```

If you now test your game, you can move the character left and right and the sprite will face the correct direction.

You can also change the subimage and animation speed through code:

```
image_index=2;
image_speed=0;
```

which would set the 3rd subimage and turn off animation.

You can manually set the angle of an image using code, such as:

```
image_angle=30;
```

If you have a moving object, you may want the image angle to match the direction, so it points in the direction it is moving. This can be done with:

```
image_angle=direction;
```

Another useful feature is a sprite strip, which may, for example, look like that shown in Figure 4-8.

Figure 4-8. *Showing a sprite strip*

You can import this as a strip and GameMaker will automatically break it down into subimages for you. Just import as shown in Figure 4-9.

Figure 4-9. *Selecting import strip image*

GameMaker should then import and crop the frames as needed, though sometimes you may need to manually enter the values. Figure 4-10 shows an imported sprite strip converted.

Figure 4-10. *Showing sprite strip converted*

A similar process can be used if you're importing a spritesheet, just set up the number of frames and frame size, as shown, for example, in Figure 4-11.

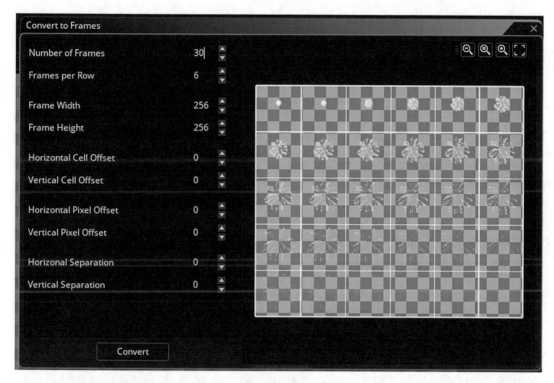

Figure 4-11. *Showing sprite sheet importing*

Basic Projects

A) Draw a sprite that rotates.

B) Make a program that draws players lives as heart images. Allow the player to press arrow keys to change lives between 1 and 6.

Advance Projects

C) Draw clouds that move across the screen at different speeds and with different alpha values.

D) Create an instance that follows a path and points in the direction it is moving.

Useful Functions

There are times when you may want an instance to slowly move to a direction. One method is:

```
speed=2;
target_direction=point_direction(x,y,mouse_x,mouse_y);
angle_diff=angle_difference(target_direction,image_angle);
image_angle+=angle_diff*0.03;
direction=image_angle;
draw_self();   draw with current settings
draw_sprite_stretched(); quick way to change size of a sprite when drawing
draw_sprite_part(); great for health / stamina bars
```

Summary

You can now do some more advanced text handling and know the basics of sprite control. You understand that animations are made of subimages that are played in sequence. You should now know how to use scaling to change which direction a sprite points in. You now are aware of how to set a subimage and change the animation speed.

CHAPTER 5

Input and Movement

Keyboard and mouse interaction is one of the key (pun intended) elements of a game. Keyboard and mouse input can be used for

- Moving a player.

- Choosing a level to play.

- Changing game options.

- Setting cheat mode.

- Switching weapons.

- Picking up items.

The following three functions can be used for checking for keyboard input:

keyboard_check() returns true each step whilst the key is being held down.

keyboard_check_pressed() will trigger once when the key is pressed.

keyboard_check_released() will trigger once when the key is released.

Place pay close attention to the preceding three functions.

Note   Pay close attention to the preceding three functions, they are distinct in nature. Failure to use the appropriate option may have undesired effect in your game.

© Ben Tyers 2023
B. Tyers, *GameMaker Fundamentals*, https://doi.org/10.1007/978-1-4842-8713-2_5

Mouse button checks work in a similar way to keyboard checks. The functions are `mouse_check_button`, `mouse_check_button_pressed()`, `mouse_check_button_released`, for example:

```
if mouse_check_button(mb_right)
{
    //This block will execute
}
```

would return true while the right button is held down.

An object instance can be moved by changing its x and y positions. x is its position in pixels across the screen, and y is how many pixels down.

For example, the following code could be placed in **Step Event** for simple movement:

```
if keyboard_check(ord("A")) {x-=2;}
if keyboard_check(ord("D")) {x+=2;}
if keyboard_check(ord("W")) {y-=2;}
if keyboard_check(ord("S")) {y+=2;}
```

or

```
if keyboard_check(vk_left) {x-=2;}
if keyboard_check(vk_right) {x+=2;}
if keyboard_check(vk_up)) {y-=2;}
if keyboard_check(vk_down) {y+=2;}
```

which would move the object around the room when a certain key is being held down.

You can also get the value of the last key that was pressed with the `keyboard_lastchar` variable. This will return the keycode of the last key that was pressed.

You could use this to get input, such as a name from the player. In the **Create Event** of an object, **obj_example** put:

```
typed="";
```

in the **Step Event** place:

```
typed=typed+keyboard_lastchar;
keyboard_lastchar="";
```

and in a **Draw Event** put:

```
draw_set_colour(c_red);
draw_text(200,200,typed);
```

This would draw what the player types onto the screen.

Basic Projects

A)   Create an object that wraps around the window if it goes off the side, and make it appear on the opposite side.

B)   Create two player objects, one moved with arrow keys, the other moved with WSAD.

Advance Project

C)   Design a maze that a player object should navigate. Prevent the player from moving through the walls.

You can check for the existence of an object:

```
if !place_meeting(x,y+2,obj_example)
{
    //do something
}
else
{
    //don't do something
}
```

will do something if the object is 1 or 2 pixels below.

Useful Functions

There are times when you may wish your game to think a player input has been performed, you can achieve this with:

```
keyboard_key_press(vk_up);
```

Which would trigger a keypress of the up arrow, forcing it to perform any code you have set up for this interaction.

```
keyboard_string();
```

Which holds the previous characters the user has typed.
A useful bit of code is;

```
keyboard_string="";
```

which would clear the typed characters.

Summary

You now know how to detect and interact with player keyboard and mouse input to make things happen. Such interaction will likely be a main feature of any game you create.

CHAPTER 6

Objects and Events

Objects are the lifeblood of GameMaker. Your game will consist of lots of objects that will interact with each other and make things happen accordingly.

- You will use objects for such things as:

- Making players and enemies move and interact

- For placing and executing code

- Checking and changing variables to make things happen

- Collision detection

- Processing mouse and keyboard input

- Drawing variables and sprites

- Creating sound effects and playing music

Objects will generally consist of several **events**. Code is placed in these events to make things happen within your game.

Note   Objects are the items in the assets of the game assets tree in the IDE. When you place an object into the room it is referred to as an instance. This is an important distinction. For example, in the resources tree, you may have an object named obj_enemy, but have three instances of it in the room, each acting as separate entity.

The most important and commonly used events will be:

© Ben Tyers 2023
B. Tyers, *GameMaker Fundamentals*, https://doi.org/10.1007/978-1-4842-8713-2_6

Create Event

This event is processed once when an instance is placed within the room (when the room starts) or upon creation using code from another object. The code may look like this:

```
/// @description example
hp=80;
motion_set(90,5);
```

which sets an initial value of hp and starts the instance moving in direction 90 at a speed of 5. It will continue moving at this speed and direction, until you tell it do something else.

Figure 6-1 shows what this code would like when placed in the **Create Event**.

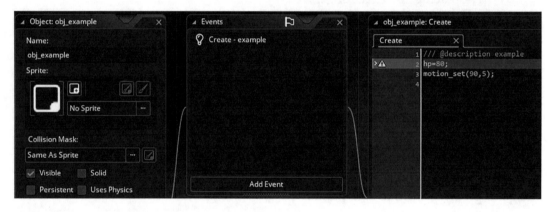

Figure 6-1. *Showing code in create event*

Mouse Events

These events trigger upon input from the mouse, such as clicking a button or scrolling the middle mouse wheel.

Note   Global mouse events allow actions to be performed if the mouse button is clicked anywhere on the screen, not just over the sprite of the object.

Standard mouse events trigger when clicked over the sprite assigned to the object (actually the mask set for the sprite).

Note   A mask is the shape/area that will be used for collision events and functions. You can set a mask as a shape using the sprite editor, for example, as shown in Figure 6-2.

Figure 6-2. *Showing a basic circle sprite mask*

The detection of mouse input can be done through GML code in a Step Event (as shown in a previous chapter), or through use of events.

Showing mouse events in Figure 6-3.

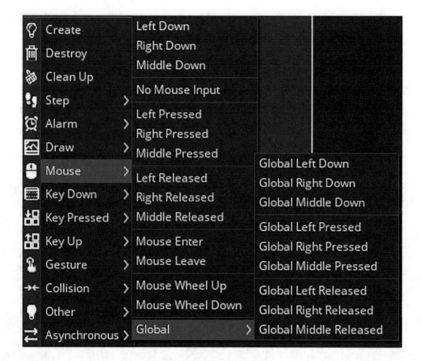

Figure 6-3. *Showing the available mouse events*

Quick Summary of the Mouse Events

Down Events – These events trigger whilst the mouse button is being held down.

Clicked Events – These trigger once when the mouse button is clicked.

Released Events – These trigger once when the mouse button is released.

Mouse Enter Event – Triggers once when the mouse enters the sprite area.

Mouse Leave Event – Triggers once when the mouse leaves the sprite.

Mouse Wheel Events – Triggers once when the mouse wheel is moved up or down.

Global Mouse Events – Work in a similar way to the top three events previously, but will trigger anywhere within the game window.

Destroy Event

This event triggers when the instance is destroyed, which can be in code from itself or set from a **Collision Event** with another object. The code for making an instance destroy itself is:

```
instance_destroy();
```

In the **Destroy Event** you could put:

```
audio_play_sound(snd_ouch,1,false);
```

This will play the sound **snd_ouch** once when the instance destroys itself.

Alarm Event

Alarms will trigger when they have counted down to 0. (They then go to -1 unless reset to a new value.)

An alarm will lose a value of 1 for each step of the game (in GameMaker there are by default 60 steps per second). So, an alarm set at 180 will trigger after three seconds. For example, the following would play a beep sound every two seconds.

Create Event:

```
alarm[0]= game_get_speed(gamespeed_fps)*2;
```

This sets the alarm to twice the room speed, which is equivalent to two seconds.

and in an **Alarm0 Event:**

```
audio_play_sound(snd_beep,1,false);
alarm[0]= game_get_speed(gamespeed_fps)*2;
```

This plays a sound then sets the alarm back to two seconds. It will countdown and repeat the sound every two seconds.

Draw Event

Your code actions for drawing should be put here, drawing text, shapes, or sprites.

If there is other code within a Draw Event you will have to tell GameMaker to draw the sprite, for example, with:

```
draw_self();
```

which will draw the currently assigned sprite and index.

Drawing order is from back to front, so in the following would draw the sprite then the text, the text will appear over the sprite, for example:

```
/// @description Draw sprite and text
draw_self();
draw_set_font(font_text);
draw_set_halign(fa_center);
draw_set_valign(fa_middle);
draw_set_colour(c_red);
draw_text(x,y,"Score "+string( score));
```

This will draw the currently assigned sprite and the text Score followed by the score.

An example would be like that shown in Figure 6-4, assuming you have added this sprite to the object.

Figure 6-4. *Drawing text above a sprite*

Step Event

With the default settings, the Step Event is processed 60 times per second. The following code would check the player's health and reduce the lives' value and reset the health. If the player is out of lives, they are taken to the room **room_game_over**.

```
if health<0
{
    lives-=1;
    health=100;
}
if lives<=0 room_goto(room_game_over);
```

This will check if the health is below 0. If it is, it reduces lives by 1 and resets health to a value of 100. If the player is out of lives (equal to 0), the player will then be taken to the room **room_game_over**.

Key Events

These events work in a similar way to the key press code shown previously in this book. You may want to use code or events, do whatever you find easiest depending upon your game setup and design. Events can make it easier to organize your code, but perhaps harder to apply any changes needed.

Note   There is nothing wrong in using keyboard events over GML code. In fact, sometimes it is preferable as it keeps your project more organized.

Figure 6-5 shows the options of Keyboard Events for keyboard interaction.

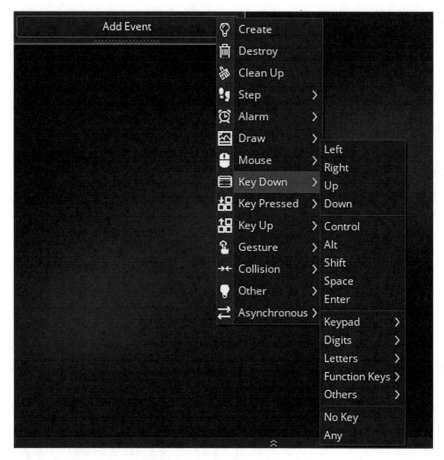

Figure 6-5. *Showing key press events*

Keyboard Events work in a similar way to **Mouse Events**, with a distinction between down, pressed, and released.

Collision Event

A Collision Event happens when two instances collide (actually, when their collision masks collide).

Upon a collision between two instances, code in the event will be executed. If you create two objects, **obj_enemy** and **obj_player** and assign them a basic sprite, you can set a **Collision Event**, as shown in Figure 6-6.

Figure 6-6. *Setting up a collision*

Some example code, for example, increasing the score by 1 for each frame the collision happens, as shown in Figure 6-7.

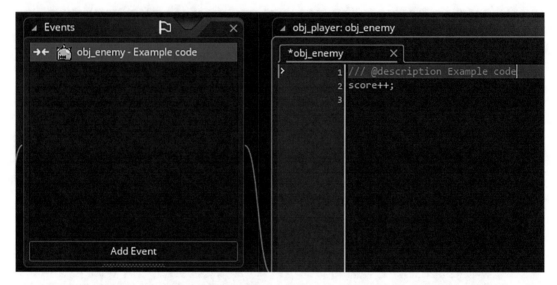

Figure 6-7. *Example collision code*

Draw GUI Event

This event draws independent of any view, and above any drawing that happens within a main draw event. It is generally used for HUD elements that do not interact with other instances in game. Some example code would be:

```
/// @description Draw hud
draw_set_colour(c_white);
draw_roundrect(50,50,1316,718,true);
draw_roundrect(70,70,270,140,true);
draw_set_font(font_text);
draw_set_halign(fa_middle);
draw_set_valign(fa_center);
draw_text(170,105,"Score "+string(score));
```

which would look as shown in Figure 6-8.

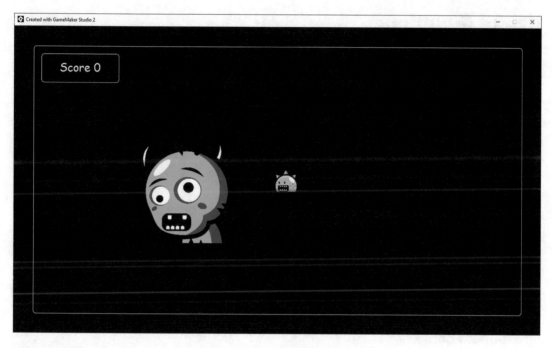

Figure 6-8. *Showing a basic hud drawn with Draw GUI*

Basic Projects

A) Allow keyboard movement of a player object. Draw health as a value over the player. Draw this health in white, changing to red when the player's health is less than 20. Allow P and L keypresses to change the health.

B) Draw text that changes color each time the spacebar is pressed.

C) Create an object that changes color when the mouse hovers over it. Use a different subimage for each color.

Advance Project

D) Create a mini game with three instances of an object. Make them move in a random direction upon start. If player clicks them, award points and move in a new random direction.

Useful Functions

You can force an event to happen, for example:

```
event_perform(ev_keypress, ord("X"));
```

which would run any code in an event set up for detecting a press of the key X. See **event_perform** in the manual for all available options.

```
event_inherited()
```

This allows the instance to inherit code from a parent object. So, for example, if you have a parent object with the following code in a **Create Event**:

```
/// @description Parent Create Event Code
size=6;
```

and the child also has a **Create Event**, you can force it to also run the parent's code, for example, with:

```
/// @description Child Create Event Code
type=8;
event_inherited();
```

It will also get the value of size from the parent.

Summary

You should now understand commonly used events and what they are used for. You should have a strong basic understanding of the code you can put in such events.

CHAPTER 7

Sprites

Sprites are images or sets of images that are that in most cases – assigned to an object. Multiple images can be shown in order to create an animation. There are several functions for drawing and manipulating sprites.

You can use sprites for

- Animation of player and enemies.

- Missiles, weapons, and other projectiles.

- Solid objects, such as walls or platforms.

- Menu options.

- Power up buttons.

- Showing lives as images.

- Trees and other in game elements.

- Collectible items.

- HUD.

- Backgrounds.

- + Most other graphical uses you can think of.

When you create a sprite, you can set its origin (an X and Y position). This is the point where the sprite will be fixed when drawing in the game. You will change this origin depending what the corresponding object will be used for.

Sprites can consist of single images or multiple images. Multiple images may be loaded in from separate images or from a sprite sheet.

Create a sprite, **spr_player** and import an image from the folder spiky land sprites.

Create an object **obj_player** and assign a sprite to it, as shown in Figure 7-1, setting the origin as middle center.

© Ben Tyers 2023
B. Tyers, *GameMaker Fundamentals*, https://doi.org/10.1007/978-1-4842-8713-2_7

Figure 7-1. *Assigning a sprite to an object*

Place the following code in the **Step Event**:

```
/// @description Simple Movement
if keyboard_check(ord("W")){y-=4;}
if keyboard_check(ord("A")){x-=4;}
if keyboard_check(ord("S")){y+=4;}
if keyboard_check(ord("D")){x+=4;}
```

Create an **obj_coins_1** and assign the coin sprite and set the origin as middle center, then place the following code in a **Collision Event** with **obj_player**:

```
x=irandom_range(16,room_width-16);
y=irandom_range(16,room_height-16);
score++;
```

When this collision event triggers, the code will move the instance to a random x and y position, within 16 pixels of the room border. It will also increase the score by 1 point.

This will look like that shown in Figure 7-2.

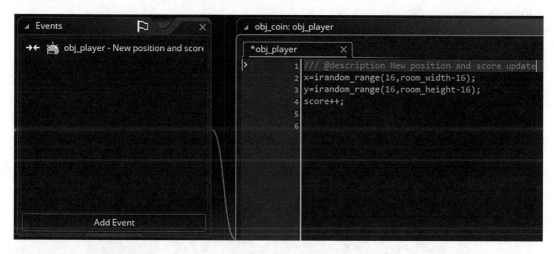

Figure 7-2. *Adding in some collision event code*

We'll also set it up so the coin only animates when the player is within 250 pixels of it. Pop the following code into a Step Event:

```
/// @description Animation control
if distance_to_point(obj_player.x,obj_player.y)<250
{
      image_speed=1;//allows animating
}
else
{
      image_speed=0;//stops animating
}
```

Place one of each object in the room room0. (which is 800x400 in size). Now test the game and collect some coins.

image_angle – Sets the direction the sprite points

Note   The default setting for a sprite is to have pointing toward the right (0 degrees). Setting sprites to this direction will make managing and controlling them much easier. 0 degrees is right, up is 90 degrees, left is 180 degrees, and down is 270 degrees.

You easily change the direction of a sprite by opening it up, clicking the appropriate editing function, as shown in Figure 7-3.

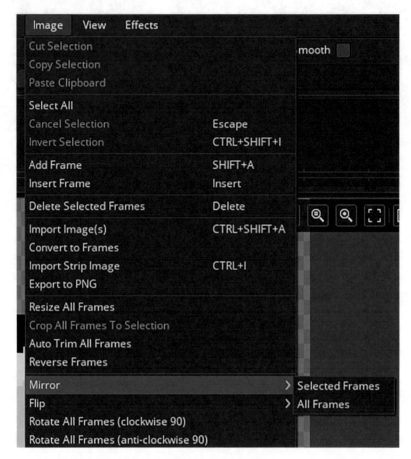

Figure 7-3. *Showing some sprite editing options*

image_speed – How quickly it animates, the default speed is 1. Setting a value of 0 would prevent the animation from happening.

Note   With default sprite and game settings, changing the animation speed of your sprite may have an undesired effect. For example, setting it to 2 would miss out every other frame. Setting to 0.5 would slow the animation down by 50%. This would of course change if you adopted the Frames Per Game setting in the Sprite Editor.

---

image_index – Can be used to set a fixed or starting subimage. If your sprite consists of four subimages, they would have the reference values of 0,1,2, and 3.

draw_sprite_ext(); – For drawing with more control. Allows you to directly set the sprite to be drawn, which subimage, its x position, its y position, x scale, y scale, image angle, color blend, and alpha value.

Start a new project and create a new object, obj_button. Create a sprite spr_button and edit its size to 300 by 100. We'll create a simple button.

Then click where shown in Figure 7-4 until you have four subimages.

Figure 7-4. *Creating additional subimages*

Then use the flood fill tool to color them yellow, green, blue, and red, as shown in Figure 7-5.

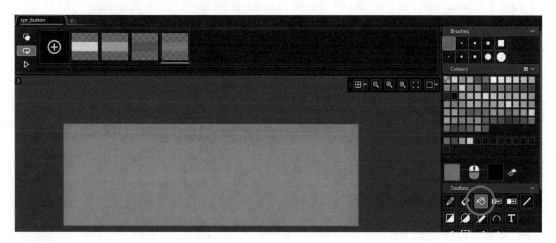

Figure 7-5. *Coloring the subimage*

Set the origin for this sprite as middle center.

Make a **Create Event** with the following code:

```
/// @description Stop animation and setup
image_speed=0;
text="mouse outside";
```

This will prevent animation and set a default message.

In the Step Event put:

```
/// @description check mouse action
//default
{
    image_index=0;
    text="mouse outside";
}
//mouse over
if position_meeting(mouse_x,mouse_y,id)
{
    image_index=1;
    text="mouse over";
}
//mouse over and left button down
if mouse_check_button(mb_left) && position_meeting(mouse_x,mouse_y,id)
{
    image_index=2;
    text="left down";
}
//mouse over and right button down
if mouse_check_button(mb_right) && position_meeting(mouse_x,mouse_y,id)
{
    image_index=3;
    text="right down";
}
```

The preceding example could be used to create an interactive element to your game, for example: setting a weapon type, taking the player to a different room, enabling or disabling game music.

You may have different sprites for moving left and right, and not moving, you could control this for example with:

```
if hspeed<0 sprite_index=spr_move_left
else
if hspeed>0 sprite_index=spr_move_right
else
sprite_index=spr_idle
```

This code checks the value of hspeed, if the value is negative then the instance is moving left, if it is positive then it is moving right. We check this value and then set the appropriate sprite. We use else statements so that if it is not moving (hspeed is equal to 0) we can set a sprite for this outcome.

Basic Projects

A)   Make an object with subimages that animates when moving. Do not animate when not moving.

B)   Make an object that animates through its subimages four times then jumps to a new position.

C)   Create a player so that the sprite points in the direction the player is moving.

Advance Project

D)   Set an object that scales in size according to its y position.

Useful Functions

You can change the sprite that an object instance is using:

```
sprite_index=spr_idle;
```

You can get the current sprite's width and height:

```
height=sprite_height;
width=sprite_width;
```

You can get the sprite's origin offset with:

```
x_pos=sprite_xoffset;
y_pos=sprite_yoffset;
```

You can also draw the sprites' bounding box, which is great for testing and debugging your game:

```
draw_rectangle(bbox_left,bbox_top,bbox_right,bbox_bottom,true);
```

Summary

You should now be able to perform basic sprites control and set subimages based upon mouse interaction.

CHAPTER 8

Health, Lives, and Score

Although most games will have different goals, most will have some kind of health, lives, or score system. GameMaker makes it easy to manage such variables by using global variables.

Note Setting health, lives, and score to have global scope allows them to be accessed by in game instance, ideal if you use a separate instance for displaying the in game HUD. If you have multiple instances of other objects in game (such as enemies) that you also want to have health, lives, or score, use instance variables such as: hp=5; my_health=75; health, lives, and score can be accessed, changed, drawn, and saved.

Note   The variables health, lives, and score have global scope, without the need to put global. before them. Note, however, in the future, they maybe redacted, so you may need to create your own global variables, as follows, for example.

I usually set the starting variables at the game start in a splash room for doing just that):

```
global.player_score=0;
global.player_health=100;
```

global.player_lives=10;You can treat all of these variables the same as you would any global variable; you can test, change, and draw these variables. The advantage of global variables is that they can be accessed from anywhere else in game.

© Ben Tyers 2023
B. Tyers, *GameMaker Fundamentals*, https://doi.org/10.1007/978-1-4842-8713-2_8

Health

This code is in a bullet's **Collision Event** with a player object:

```
health--;
instance_destroy();
```

which reduces the value of health by 1 and destroys the bullet.

Or if you are doing it within the player object with a **Collision Event** with **obj_bullet**:

```
health-=1;
with instance_destroy(other);
```

which also reduces the value of health by 1 and destroys the bullet.

Another example would be the player in a **Collision Event** with a health pack:

```
health+=10;
with (other) instance_destroy();
```

which would increase health by 10 and then destroy the pack.

You may wish to have the health set between 2 values, for example 0 and 100, say after the player collects a bonus health instance for 50 bonus health points. This can be done :

```
health+=50;
health=clamp(health,0,100);
```

keeps the health within a range of 1 and 100.

You can also draw the value of health graphically as a bar, for example:

```
draw_healthbar(x-100,y-50,x+100,y-30,(health/100)*health,c_green,c_red,
c_red,0,true,true);
```

which would draw bar centered and above the instance this code is in. It will have a width of 200 and a height of 20. This needs to be placed in a **Draw Event**.

Lives

You can draw lives as text, for example:

```
draw_text(50,50,lives);
```

This draws the value of lives as text at position 50,50.

You can also draw lives using sprites:

```
for (var i = 0; i < lives; i += 1)
{
        draw_sprite(spr_lives,0,50+(50*i),50);
}
```

This will draw the number of lives as images, evenly spaced out, as shown in Figure 8-1.

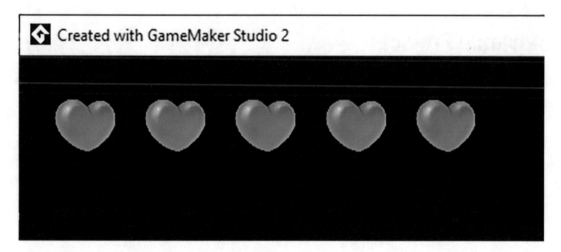

Figure 8-1. *Showing lives drawn using code*

Score

You can draw the score using code:

```
draw_text(100,40,"Your Score "+string(score));
```

which draws the text Your Score followed the value of score.

Basic Projects

A) Make a system that draws the player's health as a bar at the top of the window. Draw player's lives as images. Set up so Q and W change the health, and, A and S change the number of lives. Clamp health at a maximum of 100.

B) Make lives image change size from small to large and back. Do this through code.

Advance Projects

C) Set up a system that draws score (mod 1000) as a bar, and level as text. Increase level by 1 for every 1000 points. Allow pressing Q to increase score.

D) Set up three buttons that become active after 1000, 2000, and 3000 points. Use subimages to show if active or not, change the subimage when mouse hovers (if active). Draw a basic HUD system

Useful Functions

```
variable_global_exists()
variable_global_get()
variable_global_set()
```

Summary

You should now be able to work with lives, health, and score. You can set, change, and draw these values in an appropriate fashion.

CHAPTER 9

Mouse

Mouse input is great for a player to interact with in your game. When done well, the player can seamlessly play your game. Mouse events can be detected using code or Mouse Events. You will use mouse interaction for such things as

- Interacting with menu buttons.

- Setting a target location for a player.

- Making a gun turret point in the mouse's direction.

- Changing weapons.

- Showing info on mouse over.

- Moving a gun sight around the room.

As with keypresses, there are three main button press types:

```
if mouse_check_button(mb_left)
{
    //do something
}
```

trigger while held down

```
if mouse_check_button_pressed(mb_left)
{
    //do something
}
```

© Ben Tyers 2023
B. Tyers, *GameMaker Fundamentals*, https://doi.org/10.1007/978-1-4842-8713-2_9

trigger once when pressed

```
if mouse_check_button_released(mb_left)
{
        //do something
}
```

trigger once when released

The mouse position (in a Desktop export) is updated at the frame rate (default of 60 frames per second).

mouse_x holds the current x position.

mouse_y holds the current y position.

Both of the preceding mouse variables are global in nature, and can be accessed from any instance within your game.

There are various mouse button checks that can be made, using for example:

```
if mouse_check_button(button)
{
//do something
}
```

where **button** can be any of the following:

- mb_left

- mb_right

- mb_middle

- mb_none

- mb_any

mb_middle means middle button

mb_none means no button

mb_any means any mouse button

Mouse interaction can also be detected and acted upon using **Mouse Events**, though you will have more flexibility using code.

The following is an example:

```
if mouse_check_button(mb_left)
{
        movement_speed=10; //How quickly it moves
        target_x=mouse_x; //Where to move to on x
        target_y=mouse_y; //Where to move to on y
        x+=(target_x-x)/ movement_speed; //target position-current
        y+=(target_y-y)/ movement_speed; //target position-current
}
```

This will make the instance move slowly to the mouse's position if the left button is being held down.

You can also detect scrolling of the middle mouse wheel:

```
if mouse_wheel_up()
{
        weapon+=1;
}
```

which will Increase the value of weapon by 1 when the mouse wheel is scrolled up.
For scrolling down:

```
if mouse_wheel_down()
{
        weapon-=1;
}
```

which decreases the value of weapon by 1 when the mouse wheel is scrolled down.

Cursors

You can also set the cursor to a sprite of your choice, where sprite_name is a sprite that exists.

```
cursor_sprite=sprite_name;
```

This will remain in place until to you set it to something else.

There are times you may want to hide the cursor from view, in that case you can use:

```
window_set_cursor(cr_none);
```

which sets the cursor to invisible – remember to set it back if it is needed.

There are also several built in cursor types that can be used to great effect, see Figure 9-1.

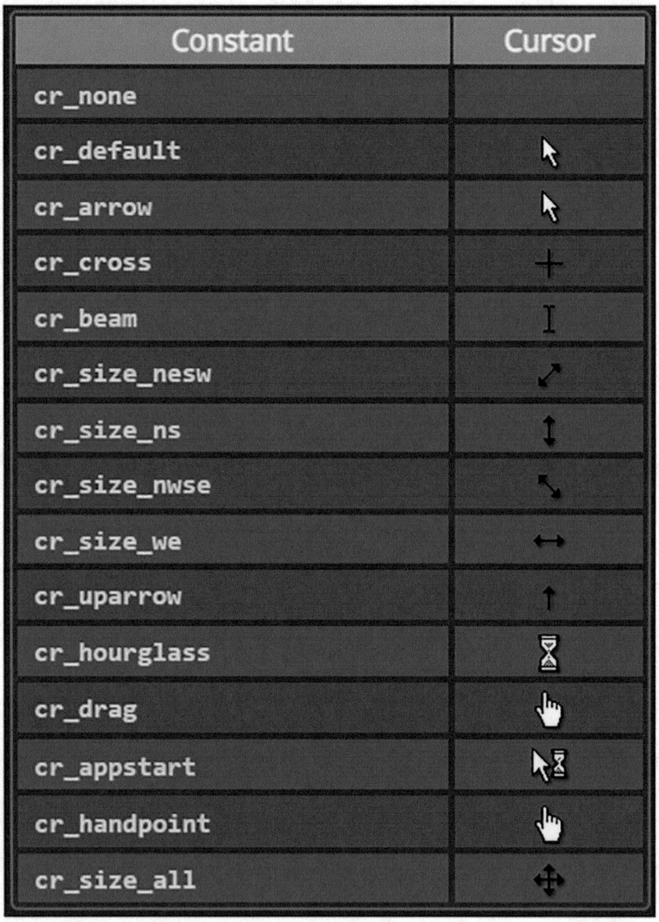

Constant	Cursor
cr_none	
cr_default	➤
cr_arrow	➤
cr_cross	+
cr_beam	I
cr_size_nesw	⤢
cr_size_ns	↕
cr_size_nwse	⤡
cr_size_we	↔
cr_uparrow	↑
cr_hourglass	⧗
cr_drag	☝
cr_appstart	➤⧗
cr_handpoint	☝
cr_size_all	✥

Figure 9-1. *Showing built in cursor types*

You can set one of these cursor types, for example with:

```
window_set_cursor(cr_arrow);
```

You can detect if the mouse cursor is over an instance, for example, the following in a Step Event:

```
if position_meeting(mouse_x,mouse_y,object_name)
{
    score++;
}
```

which increases the score if the cursor is over any instance of **obj_name** – replace with id to check if it is over itself.

Another example:

```
if position_meeting(mouse_x,mouse_y,id) &&
mouse_check_button_pressed(mb_left)
{
audio_play_sound(snd_bounce,1,false);
}
```

would check that the mouse is over itself and the left mouse button has just been clicked. A sound will then play.

Whether you use code or events, it is up to you and will change depending on what your game does.

Basic Projects

A)   Make an object that moves accordingly to mouse x position (not y position).

B)   Change the mouse's cursor when hovering over an object instance.

C)   Display the mouse's position as text on screen.

Advance Projects

D)   Set up various objects that each play a different sound when clicked.

E)   Make an object that can be clicked and dragged around the room with the mouse.

Useful Functions

You can recall the last button that was clicked:

```
if mouse_lastbutton=mb_middle
{
    y++;
}
```

Summary

You should be able to add basic mouse interaction in your own games, and allow player interaction to be acted upon.

CHAPTER 10

Alarms

Alarms can be set to a given amount of time, and then have code triggered when they trigger (reach a value of 0). Alarms have many uses, such as:

- Showing a splash screen on game start

- Setting a timer for a bomb

- Setting whether a player can be damaged or not

- Display popup text for a short period

- Change the movement of an instance periodically

- Combined to make an AI system

- Setting whether a player can shoot their weapon

An alarm can be set, for example, using:

```
alarm[0]= alarm[0]=game_get_speed(gamespeed_fps)*5; //set alarm at
5 seconds
```

Sets the alarm to five seconds.

There are 12 alarms available for each instance in you game:

```
alarm[0]
alarm[1]
....
alarm[10]
alarm[11]
```

You can set the game to execute code when an alarm triggers, by placing code in the Alarm Event as shown Figure 10-1.

© Ben Tyers 2023
B. Tyers, *GameMaker Fundamentals*, https://doi.org/10.1007/978-1-4842-8713-2_10

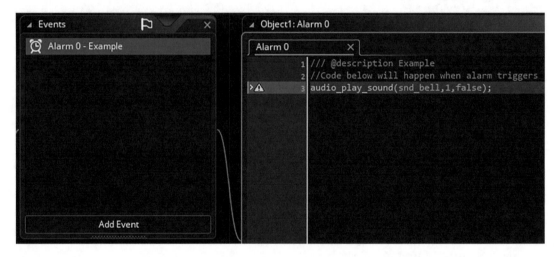

Figure 10-1. *Example code in alarm event*

You can add to an existing alarm, for example, adding ten seconds:

```
alarm[0]+= game_get_speed(gamespeed_fps)*10;
```

An example usage would be a driving game when a player picks up a fuel can. Alarms trigger when they reach 0, they then go to a value of -1. Here is an example: The following takes the player to another room after six seconds. Great for using in a splash screen at game start.

Create Event:

```
alarm[0]=6* game_get_speed(gamespeed_fps)*;
```

sets an alarm to six seconds.

Alarm[0] Event:

```
room_goto(room_title);
```

goes to the room room_title.

Delaying an Action

Another useful example is limiting how often a player can shoot their weapon:

Create Event:

```
can_shoot=true;
```

sets a flag, telling the game that the player can shoot a bullet.

When player shoots, by pressing the X key, in a **Step Event**:

```
if can_shoot && keyboard_check(ord("X"))
{
    instance_create_layer(x,y,"Instances",obj_bullet); can_shoot=false;
    alarm[1]=2* game_get_speed(gamespeed_fps)*;
}
```

checks whether the player can shoot when they press the key X. If they can, a bullet is created, the flag is changed to false and an alarm is set.

Alarm [1] Event:

```
can_shoot=true;
```

This sets can_shoot back to true so the player can shoot a bullet again.

As you can see, Alarm Events are a very useful commodity allowing us to set how often something can happen or how long something lasts.

Basic Projects

A) Make a system that displays one of ten strings for five seconds and then changes to a new string.

B) Set up an object that wraps around the screen, set it to increase speed every five seconds.

C) Make a system that plays a random sound every five seconds.

Advance Projects

D) Create a shooter system that limits to one shot every two seconds. Create a player object and a bullet object. Have the bullet shoot toward the mouse's position.

E) Set up an enemy that changes direction every five seconds, ensuring it points in the direction it is moving. Have it wrap around the room borders.

Useful Functions

You can check if an alarm is active:

```
if alarm[0]<1 active=true; else active=false;
```

You can add extra time to an alarm, for example two seconds:

```
alarm[0]+=1
```

You can turn off an alarm without triggering it:

```
alarm[0]=<0;
```

You can set and alarm to a value:

```
alarm_set(0,100);
```

You can also get the value of an alarm:

```
Remaing=alarm_get(0);
```

Summary

You can now set and control alarms to make things happen (or not) at certain periods of time. You can now limit how often a player can shoot a certain weapon.

CHAPTER 11

Collisions

Collisions are when two instances collide (actually their mask or bounding box). When these collisions happen, you can execute code.

Here are some examples of things you want to happen when a **Collision Event** takes place:

- Destroy an object, for example a projectile

- Draw a graphical effect, like an explosion

- Play a sound effect

- Change the value of the score, health, or lives – either up or down

- Set instance to move or stop moving

- Create a new instance of an object

- Execute a script

- Go to a different room

- Make the object follow a path

- Start or stop an animation

Collisions can be detected using Collision Events or code.

Figure 11-1 shows an example of a Collision Event, which would reduce the value of health by 1 for every frame that the two objects collide (60 times per second with default game settings).

© Ben Tyers 2023

B. Tyers, *GameMaker Fundamentals*, https://doi.org/10.1007/978-1-4842-8713-2_11

Figure 11-1. *Example collision event*

Collisions

You can check for any instance at a position, which will return true or false:

```
if place_empty(x,y)
{
        //do something
}
```

You can check for the collision of a specific instance with `place_meeting(x,y,object_id)`, for example:

```
if place_meeting(x,y,obj_wall)
{
        //do something
}
```

A useful bit of code that will check if the mouse cursor is over itself:

```
if position_meeting(mouse_x,mouse_y,id)
```

checks if the mouse cursor is over the instance itself (or collision mask). I use this a lot in my games.

An example usage would be the following that would set the text, depending if the mouse cursor is over the instance:

```
if position_meeting(mouse_x,mouse_y,id)
{
      text="Mouse Is Over";
}
else
{
      text="Mouse Is NOT Over";
}
```

You can destroy all instances at a given location with:

```
position_destroy(x,y);
```

The following would get the ID of an instance at a given position, or set as no one if none is present:

```
inst=instance_position(x,y,obj );
```

Another useful function is instance_place, which could be used as:

```
inst = instance_place(mouse_x,mouse_y,obj_target);
if inst !=noone
{
      score++;
}
```

which would increase the score by 1 for each frame the mouse cursor is over the object.

Note   The difference between position_meeting and place_meeting is that position_meeting allows you check for a single point, whereas place_meeting checks the collision mask. The same applies to instance_place and instance_position.

There is a major difference between instance_ and place_ functions. instance_ will return an id of an instance (or no one if no collision).

place_ will return either true or false

A common mistake is to confuse these functions, which will create undesired actions within your game.

Collision Line

Create three sprites **spr_player**, **spr_enemy**, and **spr_wall** (square in red). Edit them so they are 64x64 in size and have the origin as center. Assign these to three objects, **obj_player**, **obj_enemy** and **obj_wall**. Place the following in a **Step Event** of **obj_player**. This will provide some basic movement:

```
/// @description Basic movement
x+=4*(keyboard_check(vk_right)-keyboard_check(vk_left));
y+=4*(keyboard_check(vk_down)-keyboard_check(vk_up));
```

Make a **Draw Event** for **obj_enemy** and place the following code. This will draw itself and a line to the player if there is not a wall in the way:

```
/// @description Draw and can see check
draw_self();
draw_set_colour(c_white);
if collision_line(x,y,obj_player.x,obj_player.y,obj_wall, false,true)
== noone
{
    draw_line(x,y,obj_player.x,obj_player.y);
}
```

draws itself then a line if it can "see" the player.

Place one instance of **obj_player**, and a few each of **obj_target** and **obj_wall** into a new room and test. Figure 11-2 shows an example set up.

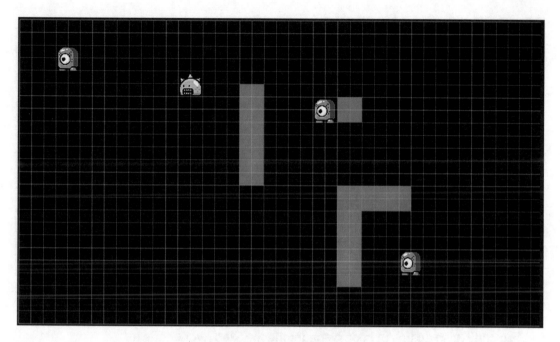

Figure 11-2. *Showing example room with objects added*

Test this now, you'll see lines drawn if the enemy and see the player.

Let's set it up so if the player collides with an enemy, the enemy is destroyed and the player gets a point.

Open up **obj_player** and create a **Collision Event** with **obj_enemy**, as shown Figure 11-3. Put the following code in this event:

```
/// @description Score & destroy
score++;
with (other) instance_destroy();
```

Figure 11-3. *Showing collision event code*

You could also do this in code by changing the **Step Event** code to:

```
/// @description Basic movement && collision detection
x+=4*(keyboard_check(vk_right)-keyboard_check(vk_left));
y+=4*(keyboard_check(vk_down)-keyboard_check(vk_up));
inst = instance_place(x,y,obj_enemy);
if_inst != noone
{
    score++;
    Instance_destroy(inst);
}
c
```

Basic Projects

A) Set the player to change sprite if it can see an enemy.

B) Make an enemy that upon collision with the player plays a sound and destroys itself.

C) Make an object that cycles through four subimages when clicked each time. Destroy when clicked on last subimage.

Advance Projects

D)   Set the player to change direction away from the mouse if the mouse gets within 300 pixels. Make this wrap around the room.

See `distance_to_point(x,y)` in the manual.

Useful Functions

You can get a list of all instances within a given radius. For example:

```
collisions=ds_list_create();
collision_circle_list(250,250,150,obj_star,false,true, collisions,true);
```

You can delete all instance at a given position:

```
position_destroy(x_pos, y_pos);
```

Note   It is important to destroy a DS list when you are done using it, this will help prevent memory leaks. For example, with `ds_list_destroy(collisions)`.

Summary

You should now be able to detect collisions, both with code and events. You can make things happen when a collision takes place.

CHAPTER 12

Rooms

Rooms are where your game takes place. This is where you place your instances for the game.

Most games will have more than one room. Rooms can be used for certain things:

- Splash Screen – Showing your logo and setting game variables

- Menu – A selection screen where player can set difficulty and play a level

- Shop – A place where a player can spend coins they have collected

- Game Levels – Where the action happens – there may be many of these

- Boss Levels – A special (usually hard) level between stages

- Game Over – Shows the player's final score

Room backgrounds can be simple, or animated, such as using a parallax effect to create depth. A parallax effect is when different background layers move at different speeds, creating an illusion of depth within your game.

You place your instances in the room, where they run and react to each other, or for example to the player's input.

Room Editor

GameMaker has a powerful room editor, allowing you to set and customize it as required.

In the room you can

- Set code that executes when the room starts.

- Set a background color, or sprite(s) as the background.

© Ben Tyers 2023
B. Tyers, *GameMaker Fundamentals*, https://doi.org/10.1007/978-1-4842-8713-2_12

- Add tiles for complex backgrounds, allow you to "paint" your level by placing individual tiles.

- Set up views (when you only want to show part of the room at a time).

- Name the room and set the dimensions.

Make a new project and load in a sprite for use as a background, and set the name as shown in Figure 12-1. Backgrounds are loaded in the same way as sprites:

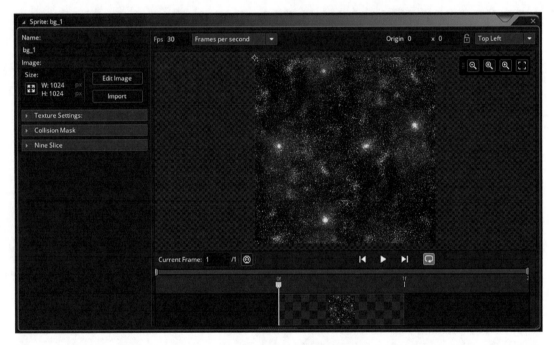

Figure 12-1. *Loading a sprite to use as a background*

Note   For naming purposes, you should use a prefix bg_ which allows you to quickly know what the asset will be used for.

Make a new room and set the background you just created, with settings shown in Figure 12-2.

Figure 12-2. *Setting a background*

You can also make the background move, for example, to the left, great if you are doing a space-shooter type game.

Change the settings to that shown in Figure 12-3.

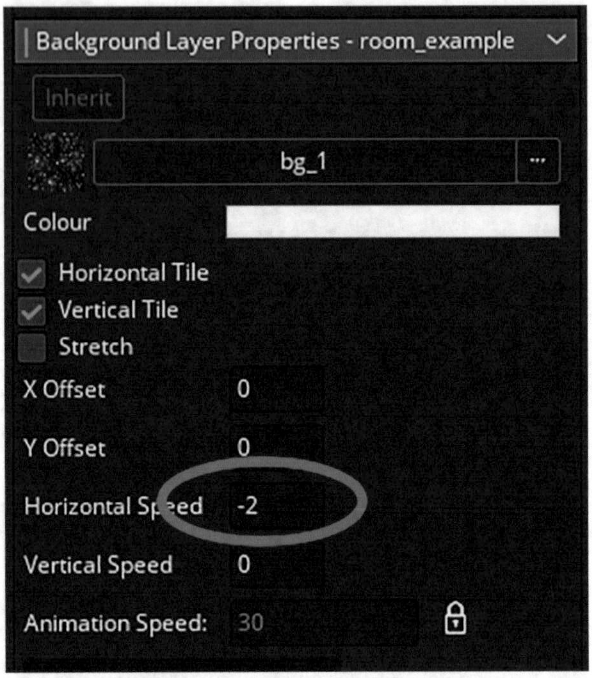

Figure 12-3. *Making a background move to the left*

If you test your game, the background will move to the left. Some commonly used code for room controls are shown in the following:

```
room_goto(room_name);
```

will go to the room with the given name.

```
room_goto_next();
```

to go to the next room (based on order in the Room Manager).

```
room_goto_previous();
```

to go to the previous room (again based on the room order).

```
room_restart();
```

restarts the room you are currently in.

Basic Projects

A) Set up a splash screen that plays a sound and then goes to the menu room after five seconds.

B) Create a menu that has three clickable objects. Clicking each one takes you to a different room.

Advance Project

C) Create two rooms, A B. Visualize them as:

A B

Make the player wrap up and down in each room. Allow player to move between them, placing the player on the correct side of the room, as shown in Figure 12-4.

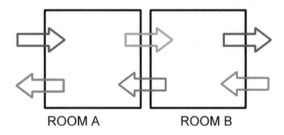

ROOM A   ROOM B

Figure 12-4. *Showing project visually*

Useful Functions

```
room_height()
room_width()
```

Both of the preceding variables return the height/width of the current room. These variables can then be used, for example, to draw a border or place instances to prevent the player from leaving the room when tied with some collision code.

Summary

You should now understand how to create and set up rooms. You understand which room will run first. You know how to traverse between rooms and set up a basic background.

CHAPTER 13

Backgrounds

Most of your rooms will have some sort of background, whether it's a solid color, a moving background, or a more complex parallax effect.

Backgrounds can be used for

- Splash screens.

- Backgrounds for levels.

- Moving backgrounds for infinite runner type games.

Backgrounds are loaded in the same way as sprites. Load in the space background from the resources and name it bg_1.

If you wanted to move the background to the left, you can set the Horizontal Speed to a negative value, for example -2, in the room settings, as shown back in Figure 12-3.

Setting Up a Background

Rename the Background layer to Background_1 and set as shown in Figure 13-1.

© Ben Tyers 2023
B. Tyers, *GameMaker Fundamentals*, https://doi.org/10.1007/978-1-4842-8713-2_13

Figure 13-1. *Setting a background*

Backgrounds can also be moved using code, which is more adaptable than using the room settings. Make an object **obj_control**, in the **Create Event** put:

```
/// @description setup
layer_y("Background_1",y);
layer_x("Background_1",x);
```

and Pop the following code into the **Step Event** of an object **obj_control**:

```
/// @description Background control
if keyboard_check(vk_up) layer_y("Background_1",y--);
if keyboard_check(vk_down) layer_y("Background_1",y++);
if keyboard_check(vk_left) layer_x("Background_1",x--);
if keyboard_check(vk_right) layer_x("Background_1",x++);
```

If you test it, you can move the background around.

Parallax Effect

Multiple backgrounds can be combined to create a Parallax Effect. This is when the foreground moves more quickly that the backgrounds.

Start a new project, and load in sprites from the asset folder Mountain Backgrounds.

Load in as shown in Figures 13-2 through Figures 13-4.

Figure 13-2. *Loading in a background*

This sprite will be used for the far background, and will move very slowly – to give a sense of depth. Additional layers can be added, for example, a mountain as shown in Figure 13-2.

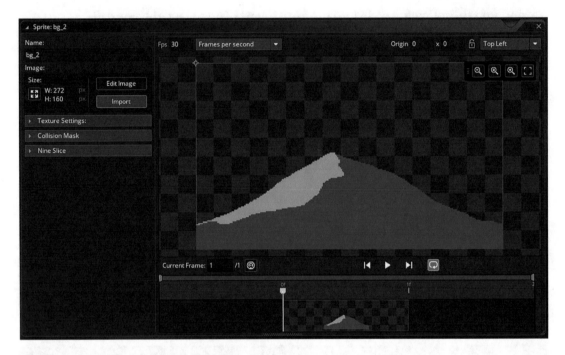

Figure 13-3. *Showing imported image bg_2*

The mountain in the preceding image will be set to move slightly faster than the rear layer, helping to increase the parallax effect.

An even nearer background, really adds to the overall effect, as shown in Figure 13-4.

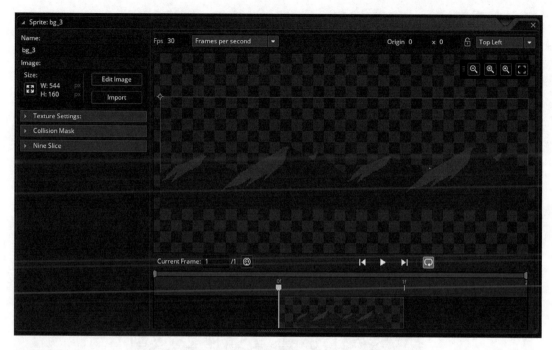

Figure 13-4. *Showing imported image bg_3*

Create some new layers and assign the matching sprite. You can click Add Background Layer, as shown in Figure 13-5 to create a new background layer.

Figure 13-5. *Creating a new background layer*

Next, name and order them as shown in Figure 13-5.

Now assign the sprites **bg_1** to **Background_1**, and similarly for **bg_2** and **bg_3**. Set **background_1** room settings, as shown in Figure 13-6.

Figure 13-6. *Settings for background_1*

Set up in a similar way with **background_2** (with Horizontal Speed of -2) and **background_3** (with Horizontal Speed of -3).

Test to see your parallax effect.

You could also do this via code by the backgrounds position, for example:

```
layer_hspeed("Background_0",25);
```

which would set Background_0 x position to 25.

Basic Projects

A) Set a system that changes background image upon pressing 1, 2, or 3.

B) Set up a tiled background that moves diagonally.

Advanced Project

C) Make the background move in the direction of the arrow keys when pressed.

D) Make a parallax with three layers, use code rather than room settings to make them move.

Useful Functions

You can make a background visible or not with:

```
bg = layer_background_get_id("Background");
layer_background_visible(bg,true);
```

which would set it to visible, false would hide this layer.

You can set the alpha of a given layer:

```
bg = layer_background_get_id("Background");
layer_background_alpha(bg,alpa_value);
```

You can scale the size of a background:

```
bg = layer_background_get_id("Background");
layer_background_xscale(bg, 2);
layer_background_yscale(bg, 2);
```

Summary

You now understand how to add backgrounds, make them move, and combine them to create a parallax effect.

CHAPTER 14

Sounds

Sounds and music within a game are very important. Using the right style of music and sound effects can alter how the player perceives the game.

Sounds can be used for

- Damage.

- Clicking menu items.

- Providing audio feedback to the play.

- Setting the scene with appropriate background music.

- Alongside graphical effects.

- Telling the player something has been done correctly.

Sound Effects

Go ahead and load in the sound snd_bell, as shown in Figure 14-1.

© Ben Tyers 2023
B. Tyers, *GameMaker Fundamentals*, https://doi.org/10.1007/978-1-4842-8713-2_14

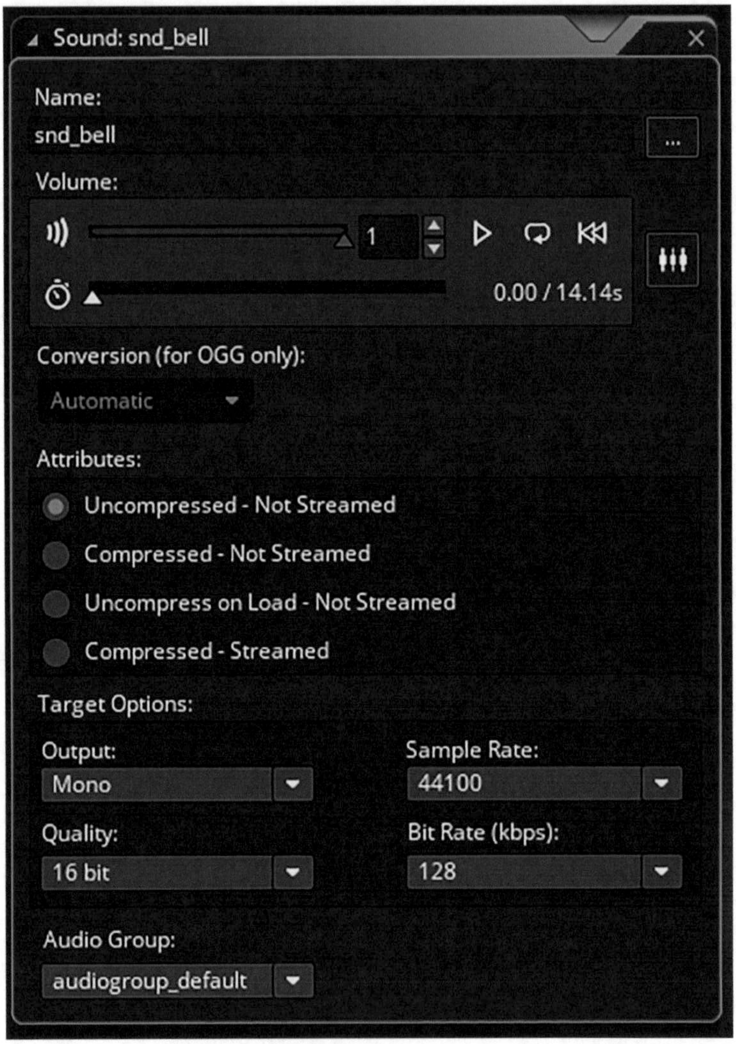

Figure 14-1. *Showing snd_bell imported*

Create an object, **obj_test** and put in the following code in a Step Event:

```
/// @description Play sound on S
if keyboard_check_pressed(ord("S"))
{
     audio_play_sound(snd_bell,1,false);
}
```

This will play the sound snd_bell each time S is pressed. The false tells the game not to loop the sound and only play it once through. Setting to true would loop the sound.

Place an instance of this object into the room and test. You'll notice that the bell will play and overlap each time you press S – which may be an undesired effect depending on how you want your game design. You have a couple of options to prevent this from happening.

Method one is to check if a sound is playing already, and if it is, don't play the sound again.

Which would look like this:

```
/// @description Play sound on S
if keyboard_check_pressed(ord("S"))
{
        if !audio_is_playing(snd_bell) audio_play_sound(snd_bell,1,false);
}
```

A second option is to stop the playing sound and play again from the beginning, which would look like this:

```
/// @description Play sound on S
if keyboard_check_pressed(ord("S"))
{
        if audio_is_playing(snd_bell) audio_stop_sound(snd_bell);
        audio_play_sound(snd_bell,1,false);
}
```

Music

Add a new sound, **snd_music_1** and load music_box from the resources.

Put the following code in to a Create Event of object **obj_test**:

```
/// @description Play music on loop
audio_play_sound(snd_music_1,1,true);
```

plays a music track on a continuous loop.

If you test now, you will hear the music playing on loop.

You can assign a sound to a variable, making it easier to refer to so you can perform actions on the sound, for example, by changing the **Create Event** code to:

```
/// @description Play music on loop
snd_bg_music=audio_play_sound(snd_music_1,1,true);
```

which would start the music and create a reference to it.

You can adjust the volume a sound plays at, for example, by adding the following in a **Step Event**:

```
if keyboard_check_pressed(ord("V"))
{
     audio_sound_gain(snd_bg_music,0.25,0);
}
```

which would change the volume of the playing to music to 25%.

Test your game and press V to change the volume.

You can check if a sound is playing, and stop it if it is. One method:

```
if keyboard_check_pressed(ord("D"))
{
     if (audio_is_playing(snd_bg_music))
     {
          audio_stop_sound(snd_bg_music);
     }
}
```

checks if key D is pressed and then stops the sound if it is playing.

Pausing and Resuming Audio

Additional commonly used functions are:

```
audio_pause_sound();
audio_resume_sound();
audio_stop_all();
```

You can add a pause and resume system with:

```
if keyboard_check_pressed(ord("P"))
{
      if audio_is_playing(snd_bg_music)
      {
            audio_pause_sound(snd_bg_music);
      }
}
if keyboard_check_pressed(ord("R"))
{
      if audio_is_paused(snd_bg_music)
      {
            audio_resume_sound(snd_bg_music);
      }
}
```

Note   If you stop a sound, it cannot be resumed. You can only resume paused audio.

Basic Projects

A) Make a basic jukebox that can select a track, pause, and resume the current track.

B) Set an object to play a random sound upon collision with a wall.

Advanced Projects

C) Play music from an object that changes volume, depending on how close the player is.

Useful Functions

You get the current track position:

```
position=audio_sound_get_track_position(snd_bg_music);
```

Conversely you can set a position:

```
audio_sound_set_position(snd_bg_music,2);
```

You can get the length of a track in seconds with:

```
track_length=audio_sound_length(snd_bg_music);
```

Summary

You can now add in sounds and music and perform basic functions such as playing, pausing, resuming, and starting. You can check whether a sound is currently playing or not.

CHAPTER 15

Splash Screens and Menu

A splash screen is typically shown when a game starts. It is a great time to show off your logo and set up variables needed for the game. This room is an ideal place to load any saved game data, such as highscores.

A menu is generally then shown, allowing the player to select which level to play. A completed game rooms tree may look something like this:

Figure 15-1. *Showing an example of rooms in the resource tree*

If you look at Figure 15-1, you'll see a house symbol next to **room_splash.** This tells you which room will be the first to run when the game is started.

Go ahead and create these rooms as shown in the Figure 15-1.

Splash Screen Example

Create a new object, **obj_splash_screen**. Assign the logo sprite from the resources folder, with the origin as Middle Center. Put the following code in the **Create Event**:

```
/// @description Set up
global.level=0;
lives=10; //Start with 10 lives
```

© Ben Tyers 2023
B. Tyers, *GameMaker Fundamentals*, https://doi.org/10.1007/978-1-4842-8713-2_15

```
score=0; //Start with a score of 0
global.bonus_score=0; //No Bonus
health=100; //Set health
alarm[0]= game_get_speed(gamespeed_fps)*5;
//center sprite
x=room_width/2;
y=room_height/2;
```

This sets some initial variables for this example.

Alarm[0] Event code will then take the player to the menu room by running the following code:

```
/// @description Change room
room_goto(room_menu);
```

Place one instance of this object in **room_splash** and test.

Basic Projects

A) Set up so a sprite animates to its last frame, set an alarm for five seconds that then goes to a new room.

B) Set a menu room and three buttons that can take a player to two levels and an info room, return to the menu when the player presses spacebar. Make the buttons change color when mouse hovers over them.

Advanced Project

C) Make five buttons that become unlocked based on the player's level. Use different subimages to graphically show this. Allow keys 1 through 5 to set current level.

Useful Functions

`room_get_name()` can be used to get the name of the current room, useful if you wish to display it on your HUD, for example. It will set a variable as string.

`room_set_camera()`

Summary

You should now understand the importance of setting up global variables at game start so you can access them later within your game.

CHAPTER 16

Random

Depending on your game's design, you want the game to play exactly the same each time it is played. Or you may want it to be different every time, for example, in matching puzzle game. This can be achieved with the random function. Randomization can be used for a lot of things such as:

- Choosing a random sound effect

- Spawning an enemy at a random location

- Adding diversity to your game

- Selecting an effect to use

- Making AI move/change direction

- Choose an attack from a selection

- Move an object to a new location

- Level generation

Depending upon the design of your game, you want things to happen in the same sequence each time the game is played, or you may want some randomness.

GameMaker will always generate the same sequence of random results.

To make testing and debugging easier, if you don't use the `randomize()` function, the game will have the sequence of randomness. Note that this does not apply to compiled games.

To force it to create different randomness, you can run the following code once at game start:

```
randomize();
```

Sets a random seed for the game.

© Ben Tyers 2023
B. Tyers, *GameMaker Fundamentals*, https://doi.org/10.1007/978-1-4842-8713-2_16

Random Numbers

In your game, you may have something in a **Create Event**:

```
/// @description Set up
starting_x=irandom(800);
starting_y=irandom(400);
```

This would set a whole random value for `starting_x` between 0 and 800 inclusive, and `starting_y` between 0 and 400.

Now each time the game is run, `starting_x` and `starting_y` will have different random values.

Make an object and put the preceding code in a **Create Event**.

In a **Step Event** put:

```
/// @description Restart room
if keyboard_check_pressed(vk_space)
{
     room_restart();
}
```

And in **Draw Event**:

```
/// @description Draw values
draw_text(200,200,"Stating X "+string(starting_x)+" Starting Y
"+string(starting_y));
```

Pop an instance of this in a room and test, each time you press spacebar, two new numbers will be chosen.

You can also choose from a sequence:

```
attack=choose(1,1,1,1,2,2,2,3);
```

This will choose a number at random. There will be a 50%(4/8) chance of getting a '1,' a 37.5%(3/8) chance of getting a '2,' and a 12.5%(1/8) chance of getting a '3'.

Other Random Uses

The preceding method is not just limited to numerical values, it can be used for colors or assets. You can, for example,

> Choose a color – my_colour=choose(c_red,c_green,c_blue);
>
> Choose a random sound – snd_explosion=choose(snd_exp_1,snd_exp_2);
>
> Deciding which enemy to spawn – enemy=choose(obj_enemy_1,obj_enemy_2);
>
> Selecting a music track – music_track=choose(snd_music_1,snd_music_2,snd_music_3);

You can choose a number at random:

number=random(50);

This will choose a random number between 0 and 50, for example: 23.476 (this could contain more digits after the decimal point).

If you are generating real numbers with decimals, the following is useful:

value=floor(8.8);

which rounds down a value, so would return 8.

value=ceil(6.7);

which rounds up a value, so would return 7.

value=round (2.7);

would return 3, as it rounds to the nearest whole number.

Often you will want to work with whole integers, this can be done with:

value=irandom(100);

This will choose a whole number integer between 0 and 100 inclusive.

You can also select a whole number within a range of numbers to choose from:

value=irandom_range(20,30);

would set a whole number between 20 and 30 inclusive.

In some games, which have the level design created randomly, you may want to set a seed to force the same sequence of random numbers. You can do this with, for example:

```
random_set_seed(123);
```

forces the seed to 123. Ideal at the start of a random level.

Basic Projects

A) Set an object that jumps to a new position upon being clicked. Ensure the new location is no closer than 50 pixels to any border.

B) Make a single instance that randomly changes direction when a random alarm event triggers. Make the instance wrap around the room.

Advanced Project

C) Set a system that chooses six random lottery numbers from 49. Draw onscreen, inside a colored circle, colored depending on the number. Allow key X to choose a new random set of balls.:

- -9 white

- 10-19 blue

- 20-29 green

- 30-39 red

- 40-49 yellow

Useful Functions

You can choose a random number within a range:

```
random_range();
```

You can also set a random seed to force a certain randomized sequence.

```
random_get_seed();
```

Summary

You'll have the ability to create variation within your game using various random functions.

CHAPTER 17

AI

Most games will have an enemy that exhibits some basic AI (Artificial Intelligence). This chapter serves as an introduction to some basic AI.

Some of the functions the AI may have:

- Avoid the player
- Guard an area and attack the player if they get too close
- Calculate the best play in a card game
- Shoot a projectile at the player
- Shoot at a player if they see them

Generally, you will evaluate some code and determine if it is true or false (or some other value) and make something happen as a result.

This section will start with a basic system and will add more features in stages.

Make three very basic sprites (32x32 in size) **spr_wall**, **spr_player** and **spr_enemy**, set the origin as center, then assign them to **obj_wall**, **obj_player**, and **obj_enemy**.

Open up **obj_player** and place the following code in its **Step Event**:

```
/// @description movement
var hor=4*keyboard_check(vk_right)-keyboard_check(vk_left);
var vert=4*keyboard_check(vk_down)-keyboard_check(vk_up);
if !position_meeting(x+hor+(sign(hor)*16),y,obj_wall)
{
    x+=hor;
}
if !position_meeting(x,y+vert+(sign(vert)*16),obj_wall)
{
    y+=vert;
}
```

© Ben Tyers 2023
B. Tyers, *GameMaker Fundamentals*, https://doi.org/10.1007/978-1-4842-8713-2_17

The preceding code will provide basic movement and prevent the player moving through a wall object.

Basically the code uses a key press and that there is not a wall in the way, if there is not, then it's position is changed. sign(value) returns -1 for a negative value and 1 for a positive value. It is not perfect, but it will suffice for testing.

An example usage of sign() would be for setting the image_xscale of an instance so it points to the correct direction when moving left or right.

For example, the following in a **Step Event**:

```
/// @description Example
if keyboard_check(vk_left)
{
     hspeed=-2;
}
if keyboard_check(vk_right)
{
     hspeed=2;
}
dir=sign(hspeed);
image_xscale=dir;
```

Set up the room like that shown in Figure 17-1.

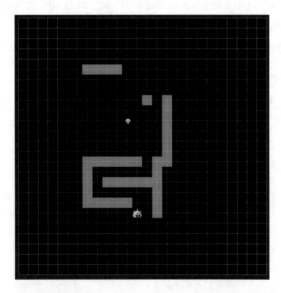

Figure 17-1. *Example room set up*

Check the movement works by testing.

Basic Enemy AI

Next, we'll set up an **enemy obj**, place the following in its **Create Event**:

```
/// @description Set Flag
can_see=false;
```

This code will set an initial flag. We'll use and change this when the enemy can or can't see the player.

In the **Step Event** of this object, put the following code. This will check for a line of sight to the player. If the player is not hidden behind a wall, the enemy will move toward the player:

```
/// @description if there is a direct line of sight  to the player
if (collision_line(x, y,obj_player.x,obj_player.y, obj_
wall,true,false))    !=noone
{
     can_see=false;
}
else
{
     can_see=true;
     mp_potential_step_object(obj_player.x, obj_player.y, 5, obj_wall);
}
```

Finally create a **Draw Event** for this object with the following code, just for testing:

```
/// @description Drawing code
draw_self();
if can_see
{
     if distance_to_object(obj_player)>2 mp_potential_step (obj_
     player.x,obj_player.y,2,true);
}
```

This will draw its own sprite, and a line between itself and player if can_see is true.

Load **snd_ouch** from the resources.

Place the following in **obj_enemy** with a Collision Event with **obj_player**:

```
/// @description Play audio
audio_play_sound(snd_ouch,1,false);
instance_destroy();
```

The preceding code will play the sound snd_ouch upon collision with the obj_player, and then destroy itself.

Place a few extra instances of **obj_enemy**, as shown in Figure 17-2 and test so far.

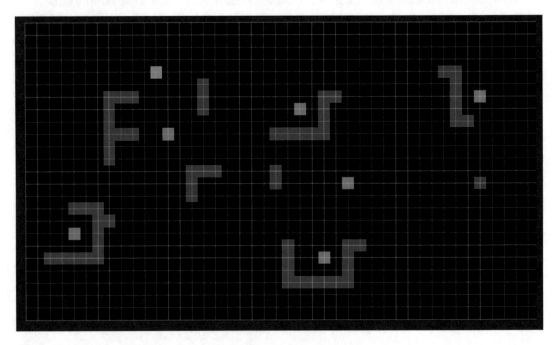

Figure 17-2. *Showing additional obj_enemy added*

Enemy Shooting

Next create a sprite **spr_bullet** from the resources, rotate, and set the size as 32x13 as shown in Figure 17-3.

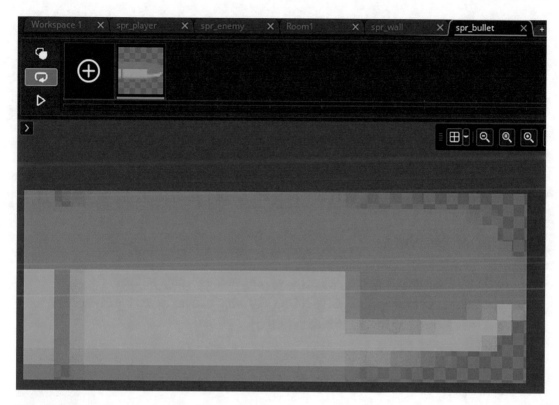

Figure 17-3. *Setting up a bullet sprite*

Assign this sprite an object **obj_bullet**.

Put this code in a **Collision Event** with **obj_player**:

```
/// @description On collision
audio_play_sound(snd_ouch,1,false);
instance_destroy();
```

plays a sound and destroys itself upon collision with obj_player

Change the Create Event of **obj_enemy** to:

```
/// @description Set Flag
can_see=false;
can_shoot=true;
```

sets an additional flag for shooting control

Change the Step Event of **obj_enemy** to:

```
/// @description if there is a direct line of sight  to the player
```

```
if (collision_line(x, y,obj_player.x,obj_player.y, obj_
wall,true,false))    !=noone
{
      can_see=false;
}
else
{
      can_see=true;
      mp_potential_step_object(obj_player.x, obj_player.y, 5, obj_wall);
}
if can_see && can_shoot
{
      bullet=instance_create_layer(x,y,"Instances",obj_bullet);
      bullet.direction=point_direction(x,y,obj_player.x,obj_player.y);
      bullet.image_angle=bullet.direction;
      bullet.speed=5;
      can_shoot=false;
      alarm[0]=room_speed*3;
}
```

Finally, pop in an **Alarm[0] Event** with the following:

```
/// @description Allow shooting again
can_shoot=true;
```

Set flag so it can shoot again.

Now test the game, if an enemy has a line of sight to the player, it will shoot a bullet every three seconds.

Basic Projects

A) Set an instance that moves randomly left and right across the top
    of the window (wrapping as needed). Set it to drop a collectible
    object every five seconds. Player to collect these items. Draw a
    basic HUD on screen.

B) Set up a player that can be moved with arrow keys. Set an enemy
    to shoot projectiles at the player, getting more frequent as the
    player gets closer. Destroy projectile when outside room.

Advanced Projects

C) Set an enemy that changes direction every five seconds away from
    the player.

Useful Functions

collision_rectangle(); Allows you to get a list of all instances in a gen area
   collision_line_list(); Returns all instances that collide with a line
   point_in_circle(); Return instances within a circular region
   point_in_rectangle(); Return true or false, depending on whether a given
coordinate falls in an area
   point_in_triangle(); Returns instances within a triangular region

Summary

You now know some basic functions to make enemies react to player input and
positions. You can gradually build upon this to create more complex enemy interactions.

CHAPTER 18

INI Files

If you have a game that people will play for a few minutes at a time, you will want to save certain data so that they can continue the next time they play. Things you will want to save may include

- Player's name, health, lives, and score.

- Any previous highscore.

- The total distance they have moved.

- How many bullets have been fired.

- What keys they have collected.

- Which treasure chests have been opened.

- Which enemies have been defeated.

INI File Contents

An easy way to save and load data is with INI files. INI files consist of two main elements:
[sections] and keys
A simple ini file would look like this:

```
[player]
highscore=1000
name="Ben"
```

Note On most exports, it is not required to include an INI as an included file. You can set this as a text file with the required section, keys and values.

© Ben Tyers 2023
B. Tyers, *GameMaker Fundamentals*, https://doi.org/10.1007/978-1-4842-8713-2_18

Loading Data

To load data from this file you can use

```
ini_open("savedata.ini");
global.highscore=ini_read_real("player","highscore", 0);
global.player_name=ini_read_string("player","name","None");
ini_close();
```

This code will open the INI file and set two global values that can be used in game, using the data that is stored in it.

If no INI file exists (or a section/key is not present), for example, it is the first time the game has been played, then the values would have the default values set to them, in this case global.highscore would be set to 0 and global.player_name as "None." The default value is after the last, . If the INI file exists, then the saved value will be set.

Saving Data

Writing a value to an INI is just as easy:

```
ini_open("savedata.ini");
ini_write_real("levels_completed","level",global.levels);
ini_write_string("player","name",global.player_name);
ini_close();
```

This opens an ini file and writes data to it, overwriting, and sections and keys, if already present. The file is then closed.

Note   Open the INI files, read or write data, and then close it when done; leaving an INI file open can lead to issues.

After saving these values, the INI file may look like this:

```
[levels_completed]
level=14
[player]
"name"="Richard"
```

128

ini_read_real() and ini_write_real() are used with reals and integers.

ini_read_string() and ini_write_string() are used with strings.

Basic Projects

A) Set a splash room to load any saved data. If data is present, set the player to the saved location upon game room starting. Make a player that can be moved using arrow keys. Upon pressing x, save the players location and restart the game.

B) Set a counter that saves how many times the spacebar has been pressed. Set it to save/load as needed.

Advanced Project

C) Make a system that saves five players' info: name, age, favorite food. Upon game start, offer to display saved data (if present) or create new data.

Useful Functions

You can check if a key or section exists:

```
ini_section_exists();
ini_key_exists();
```

for example, with an open ini file

```
if !ini_section_exists("Level_1")
{
    ini_write_real("Level_1", "Complete", true);
}
```

You can delete the whole ini file with:

```
if file_exists("game_data.ini")
{
    file_delete("game_data.ini ");
}
```

Summary

You now understand the structure of an INI file and how to write and read data. You should now be able to make a basic save system to save a players game progress.

CHAPTER 19

Effects

Graphical effects are important in most games. Whether it's just a little sparkle effect or an explosion. Graphical effects can be done using sprites, built-in effects, or the Effects layers. The built-in effects allow for quick prototyping of a game, and can even be used in a finished project. Some examples would be

- Visually showing the player that a button has been pressed.

- Showing damage when hit by a bullet.

- Explosion when an enemy dies.

Effects

A number of basic effects can be created with just one line of code, for example:

```
/// @description Simple effect
effect_create_above(ef_spark,mouse_x,mouse_y,2,c_white);
```

This would a create a spark effect at the mouse's position.

Create an object **obj_test** and put this code in a **Step Event**, pop it into a room and test.

The general format used is:

```
effect_create_below(type,x,y,size,colour);
```

Note   Effect code does not need to be in a Draw Event, it can be in a Step Event, Key Press Event, etc. which can be very useful!

© Ben Tyers 2023
B. Tyers, *GameMaker Fundamentals*, https://doi.org/10.1007/978-1-4842-8713-2_19

You'll see that there are two options: effect_create_above() and effect_create_below(). The above option will draw above it's default sprite or anything in its **Draw Event**, while below would draw beneath.

Another example would be that below, add this to your **Step Event** and test again:

```
if mouse_check_button_pressed(mb_left)
{
    effect_create_above(ef_explosion,mouse_x,mouse_y,2,c_red);
}
```

This creates an explosion effect each time the left mouse button is clicked.

There are several effects to choose from:

- ef_cloud

- ef_ellipse

- ef_explosion

- ef_firework

- ef_flare

- ef_rain

- ef_ring

- ef_smoke

- ef_smokeup

- ef_snow

- ef_spark

- ef_star

Try out some of these effects now, by editing the code in your **Step Event**.

Using randomness, you can create some cool effects. Try the following and see what it does:

```
if mouse_check_button_pressed(mb_left)
{
    effect_create_above(ef_flare,mouse_x,mouse_y,1,choose(c_blue,
    c_purple,c_green));
}
```

This will create a flare effect with a random color of blue, purple, or green, while the right button is being held down.

Now try this code:

```
if mouse_check_button_released(mb_left)
{
effect_create_above(choose(ef_spark,ef_smoke,
ef_explosion, ef_firework),mouse_x,
mouse_y,2,choose(c_white,c_grey));
}
```

which creates a random effect in white or grey.

Figure 19-1 shows these effects in action.

Figure 19-1. *Showing standard effect*

Effect Layer

You can also create effects using the Effect Layer. A number of effects are available, with new ones added on a regular basis.

Start a new project, load in the ocean background and set it as a background for a room, as shown in Figure 19-2.

Figure 19-2. *Assigning a sprite as a background*

Next, add an **Effect Layer** between the Instances and **Background** layers by clicking, as shown in Figure 19-3. The Effect Layer applies to layers below it, so in this case, the effects would be applied to **Background** and not **Instances** above it.

Figure 19-3. *Adding an effect layer*

Now choose an effect, for example as shown in Figure 19-4.

Figure 19-4. *Choosing an effect*

Have a play around choosing various settings for each effect, for example, as shown in Figure 19-5.

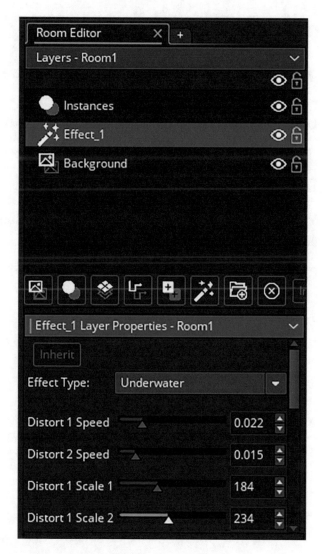

Figure 19-5. *Trying out various effects and settings*

Basic Projects

A)   Set key S & R to change the weather between snow and rain.

B)   Create fireworks in random size and color.

Advance Projects

C)   Use the effects layer to create an underwater scene with wave effects.

D)   Make a system that shakes the room when space is help down.

Useful Functions

Pre-rendered sprite animations can also be used to create some awesome effects, for example, a sprite sheet with explosions, as shown in Figure 19-6.

Figure 19-6. *Showing a sprite explosion sheet*

GameMaker also allows use of a particle system; if you're feeling adventurous, then look into this.

fx_* functions allow controlling the effects layer whilst your game is running.

Summary

You can now perform basic effects, both in code and using effects layers.

CHAPTER 20

Loops

A common need in programming is to repeat the same code multiple times. This functionality is available through using loops. There are four main loop functions in GML: do, while, for, and repeat. Each of these has its own strengths and weaknesses.

Loops are great for

- Processing data in ds lists or arrays.

- Performing the same action multiple times.

- Performing a calculation until it is true.

- Drawing data from lists, grids, or arrays.

A loop can result in many similar actions being executed in a very short time.

Note It is important to make certain that loops run the correct number of times and then stop. It is possible through a coding mistake to create an infinite loop that runs forever. This will cause the game to stop working. Care needs to be taken to avoid this from happening.

Also note that a loop will complete itself within one frame of the game. If you are using large loops or using lots at a time, another approach may be required. For example, if you looped through a block of code 1000 times within a single frame, it may have undesired effects such as making your game stutter.

© Ben Tyers 2023
B. Tyers, *GameMaker Fundamentals*, https://doi.org/10.1007/978-1-4842-8713-2_20

Repeat Loop

repeat can be used to process the same code block several times at once. For example:

```
repeat(5) //Will repeat the following block five times
{
    effect_create_above(ef_firework,100,100,2,choose(c_white,c_yellow,
    c_green,c_blue));
}
```

which would create five firework effects at once.

While Loop

A while loop will repeat until an expression is true or not true, for example:

```
while !place_free(x,y)
{
    x = random(room_width);
    y = random(room_height);
}
```

This would repeat until a free space is found.

Note   Ensure this loop will exit (complete) at some point, if not it will run continuously and freeze your game. As in the preceding example, ensure there are free places within the room.

For Loop

A for loop is used when you want to increment a value and perform an action. For example, in the following, where it will populate an array with the values 0 to 24 inclusive.

```
for (var i=0;i<25;i++)
```

```
{
    array[i]=i;
}
```

The preceding code will loop from 0 to 24 and then exit. It will place the numbers 0 to 24 within the array.

If you wanted to include the value 25 in the loop you can use: i<=number

For example:

```
for (var i=0;i<=25;i++)
{
    array[i]=i;
}
```

which would populate the array with values 0 to 25 inclusive.

You could draw the contents in reverse order with

```
for (var i=25;i>=0;i--)
{
    draw_text(200,20+(25*i),array[25-i]);
}
```

Do Loop

Like a while loop, but will execute at least once until an expression returns as true:

```
do
{
    x = random(room_width);
    y = random(room_height);
}
until (place_free(x,y));
```

will try random positions until a free space is found.

Note   The do loop will always execute at least once, but in for or while, it can be skipped.

Basic Projects

A) While loop. Set an object that randomly chooses a random position within 100 pixels of another object. Allow spacebar to find a new location.

B) For loop. Make a list with 100 numbers in random order from 1 to 1000. Display this data on screen in four columns, in ascending order. Allow spacebar to choose a new set.

Advance Projects

C) Set four random points in the room. Make an object visit each of these locations. Spacebar to restart.

D) Make a system that takes in all the names of students in your class. Display onscreen in alphabetical order, one at a time every five seconds.

Useful Functions

If you want to gradually increase a value, you can use something like:

```
variable++;
```

In a Step Event

```
break
```

There will be times when you may wish to exit a loop early, for example, when a certain condition or value is met. break allows to do this.

Summary

You now are now aware of some appropriate uses of loops and how they can be implemented. You understand how to add, change, process, and display data.

CHAPTER 21

Arrays

Arrays are an ideal way to store organized data, such as:

- Keeping track of player's weapons, whether available, and how many they have

- Storing names and associated data, like height or birthday

Arrays can hold an assortment of data and is not limited to variables. You can store sprite names, sounds, instance ids, and more.

Array Example

An example of 1-dimensional array, holding the names of some planets:

```
planet[0]= "Mercury";
planet[1]= "Venus";
planet[2]= "Earth";
planet[3]= "Mars";
planet[4]= "Jupiter";
planet[5]= "Saturn";
planet[6]= "Uranus";
planet[7]= "Neptune";
```

This places planet names as strings into an array.

In table format, this would look as shown in Table 21-1.

© Ben Tyers 2023
B. Tyers, *GameMaker Fundamentals*, https://doi.org/10.1007/978-1-4842-8713-2_21

Table 21-1. *Visualization of preceding data in an array*

Position Value	Contents
0	"Mercury"
1	"Venus"
2	"Earth"
3	"Mars"
4	"Jupiter"
5	"Saturn"
6	"Uranus"
7	"Neptune"

Note   Like most data structures in GameMaker, the first index is 0, so an array with 10 values would have the locations of 0 through 9.

You can access and draw one value, for example, the value at position 2:

```
draw_text(100,100,planet[2]);
```

which would draw "Earth" at position 100,100.

You can use a 2D array to store more info.

Note   The different cells can have a mixture of data types, for example, strings, numbers, or resource IDs.

Put the following in a **Create Event of** a new object, called **obj_example:**

```
/// @description Set and Populate Array
//names
planet[0][0]= "Mercury";
planet[0][1]= "Venus";
planet[0][2]= "Earth";
planet[0][3]= "Mars";
planet[0][4]= "Jupiter";
```

```
planet[0][5]= "Saturn";
planet[0][6]= "Uranus";
planet[0][7]= "Neptune";
//size
planet[1][0]= 4879
planet[1][1]= 12104
planet[1][2]= 12742
planet[1][3]= 6779
planet[1][4]= 139822
planet[1][5]= 116464
planet[1][6]= 50724
planet[1][7]= 49244
//Colours
planet[2][0]= "Gray";
planet[2][1]= "Pale Yellow";
planet[2][2]= "Blue & White";
planet[2][3]= "Red";
planet[2][4]= "Orange";
planet[2][5]= "Gold";
planet[2][6]= "Pale Blue";
planet[2][7]= "Blue";
```

This places planet names and info into a 2-dimensional array.

Drawing Array Contents

As the array code is neatly organized, you can draw the values on screen using a method known as a nested loop:

```
/// @description Draw array contents
for (var i=0;i<3;i++)
{
    for (var j=0;j<8;j++)
    {
        draw_text(150+i*150,j*30,planet[i][j]);
    }
}
```

This draws the contents of the array in a nice grid on screen as shown in Figure 21-1.

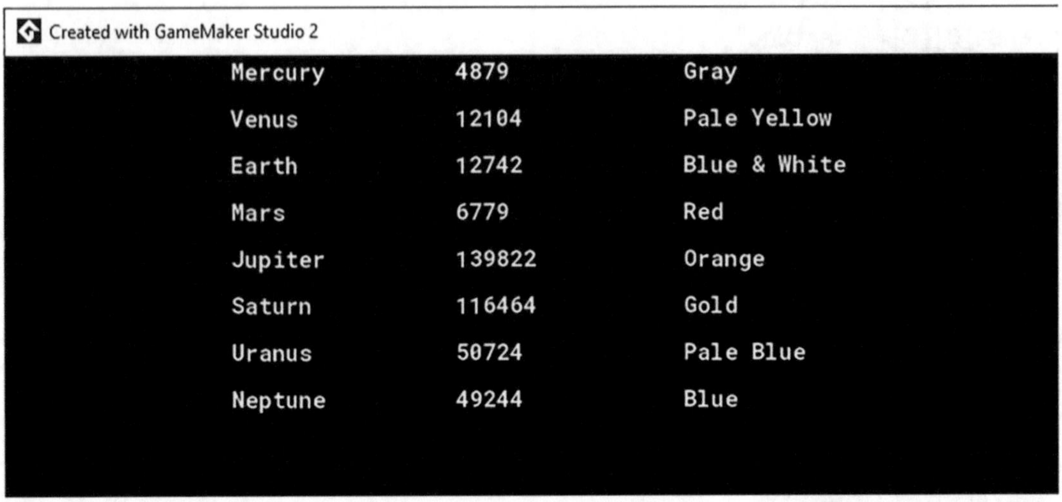

Figure 21-1. *Showing data drawn to screen*

An example project file is available in the resources folder: Project Example Solutions file Chapter 21 A

You can compare array values:

```
if planet[1,0]>planet[1,1]
{
    text_to_show=(planet[0,0]+ " is bigger than "+ planet[0,1]);
}
else
{
    text_to_show=(planet[0,0]+ " is smaller than "+ planet[0,1]);
}
draw_text(400,400,text_to_show);
```

which sets text_to_show depending on which planet is bigger.

You can add this to the **Draw Event** and test this now.

Array-Based Shop

A real example that you may use in game is for storing and processing weapon info. For example, you could populate an array with the data in Table 21-2.

Table 21-2. *Representation of 2-dimensional array*

Name	Power	Cost	Starting Amount	Sound	Gun Sprite	Bullet Object
"Gun"	1	1	200	snd_gun	spr_gun	obj_bullet_gun
"MachineGun"	5	10	400	snd_mach_gun	spr_mach_gun	obj_bullet_mach_gun
"RocketGrenade"	250	300	8	snd_rocket	spr_rocket	obj_bullet_rocket
"Nuke"	1000	5000	2	snd_nuke	spr_nuke	obj_bullet_nuke

You can create a data array for the previous table in code using

```
/// @description Put data in array
global.cash=100000;
global.selected_weapon=0;
///declare array
//weapon name
weapon_info[0][0]="Gun";
weapon_info[0][1]="Machine Gun";
weapon_info[0][2]="Rocket Grenade";
weapon_info[0][3]="Nuke";
//weapon strength
weapon_info[1][0]=1;
weapon_info[1][1]=5;
weapon_info[1][2]=250;
weapon_info[1][3]=1000;
//weapon cost
weapon_info[2][0]=1;
weapon_info[2][1]=10;
weapon_info[2][2]=300;
```

```
weapon_info[2][3]=5000;
//weapon ammo
weapon_info[3][0]=200;
weapon_info[3][1]=400;
weapon_info[3][2]=8;
weapon_info[3][3]=2;
//weapon sound effect
weapon_info[4][0]=snd_gun;
weapon_info[4][1]=snd_mach_gun;
weapon_info[4][2]=snd_rocket;
weapon_info[4][3]=snd_nuke;
//weapon sprite
weapon_info[5][0]=spr_gun;
weapon_info[5][1]=spr_mach_gun;
weapon_info[5][2]=spr_rocket;
weapon_info[5][3]=spr_nuke;
//weapon bullet object
weapon_info[6][0]=obj_bullet_gun;
weapon_info[6][1]=obj_bullet_mach_gun;
weapon_info[6][2]=obj_bullet_rocket;
weapon_info[6][3]=obj_bullet_nuke;
```

which populates a 2-dimensional array with various weapons data shown in Table 21-2.

Create an object, **obj_example**, make a **Create Event** and put in the preceding code.

Create the objects, import the sounds and sprites, and name them accordingly. Add the following to the **Create Event** for each bullet object:

```
/// @description For testing
hspeed=3;
```

There is a project file for this example in the resources projects folder, named **Chapter 21 B**, which has all the assets loaded in to make testing quicker for you.

A simple weapon select system can be put in the **Step Event:**

```
///@description Control
if keyboard_check_pressed(ord("0"))
{
```

```
        global.selected_weapon=0;
}
if keyboard_check_pressed(ord("1"))
{
        global.selected_weapon=1;
}
if keyboard_check_pressed(ord("2"))
{
        global.selected_weapon=2;
}
if keyboard_check_pressed(ord("3"))
{
        global.selected_weapon=3;
}
if mouse_check_button_pressed(mb_left) && weapon_info[3][global.selected_
weapon]>=1//check for available ammo
{
    audio_play_sound(weapon_info[4][global.selected_weapon],10, false);
    //play firing sound
    weapon_info[3][global.selected_weapon]-=1;//reduce ammo
    instance_create_layer(mouse_x,mouse_y,"Instances",weapon_info[6]
    [global.selected_weapon]);//create bullet
}
x=mouse_x;
y=mouse_y;
```

Weapon control example. Allows selection of weapons with numerical keys. Upon mouse click, it plays the appropriate weapon sound and creates an instance of that weapon at the mouse cursor position.

In a **Draw Event** put:

```
/// @description drawing
draw_sprite(weapon_info[5][global.selected_weapon],0,x,y);
//draw info
draw_text(10,20,"Strength:"+string(weapon_info[1][global.selected_
weapon]));
```

```
draw_text(10,40,"Cost:"+string(weapon_info[2][global.selected_weapon]));
draw_text(10,60,"Current Ammo:"+string(weapon_info[3][global.selected_
weapon]));
```

displays weapon info on the screen.

You could also make a simple shop system, allowing the player to purchase weapons.

From **obj_example**, delete the Step and **Draw Events**, but leave the **Create Event** code.

Add the following into a **Step Event**:

```
///@description Shop Control

if keyboard_check_pressed(ord("0"))
{
    if global.cash>=weapon_info[2][0]
      {
            global.cash-=weapon_info[2][0];
            weapon_info[3][0]++;
      }
}

if keyboard_check_pressed(ord("1"))
{
    if global.cash>=weapon_info[2][1]
      {
            global.cash-=weapon_info[2][1];
            weapon_info[3][1]++;
      }
}
if keyboard_check_pressed(ord("2"))
{
    if global.cash>=weapon_info[2][2]
      {
            global.cash-=weapon_info[2][2];
            weapon_info[3][2]++;
      }
}
```

```
if keyboard_check_pressed(ord("3"))
{
    if global.cash>=weapon_info[2][3]
      {
            global.cash-=weapon_info[2][3];
            weapon_info[3][3]++;
      }
}
```

which detects a keypress and then checks enough cash is available; if there is, it deducts cash accordingly and increases the current value of available weapons.

And a **Draw Event** to draw the data:

```
/// @description drawing
draw_text(80,80,"Cash "+string(global.cash));
for (var weapon=0; weapon<4; weapon+=1)
{
    yy=150+(150*weapon);
    draw_sprite(weapon_info[5][weapon],0,150,yy);
    draw_text(220,yy,"Type "+weapon_info[0][weapon]);
    draw_text(420,yy,"Cost "+string(weapon_info[2][weapon]));
    draw_text(550,yy,"Amount "+string(weapon_info[3][weapon]))
}
```

Basic Projects

A) Using code, make an array that holds data of your fellow students. Display this on screen.

B) Populate an array with ten foods, randomly display one every five seconds.

Advanced Projects

C)   Make an array that holds the starting locations of pieces in a chess game, use a different letter for each piece, use uppercase for black and lower case for white. Draw this data onscreen.

Useful Functions

You can get the size of an array, for example:

```
size=array_length(example);
```

You can add to the end of an array with:

```
array_push(names,"Steve");
```

You can create an array and populate with default values, for example, the following, which would create 50 entries with a value of 12.

```
new_array=array_create(50,21);
```

It also possible to insert a value into an array and shift the cells down, for example:

```
array_insert(0,10);
```

which would add a new value of 10 at position 0.

Summary

After completing this chapter, you can now populate an array with data, access, and display this data. You are now aware how to change data held in a multidimensional array and create a basic weapon management system.

CHAPTER 22

DS Lists

Data Structures (DS) are similar in nature to arrays, but you can do so much more with them!

You can do things such as:

- Sort names (or other strings) alphabetically, numbers, and more – descending or ascending

- Store a player inventory

- Shuffle lists randomly

- Manage and queue up audio or graphical effects

- Message management

- Store and process lists of numbers

- Remove an item, and the list will reorganize itself

- Works with variables, ids, sprites, objects, etc.

- Process commands in order

- Insert contents anywhere on the list

- Search a list for an element

Creating a DS List

It is relatively easy to create a `ds_list`:

```
example_list = ds_list_create();
```

This tells GameMaker that this variable `example_list` is a ds list.
Then can it add some contents

```
ds_list_add(example_list,"Earth");
ds_list_add(example_list,"Mars");
ds_list_add(example_list,"Jupiter");
ds_list_add(example_list,"Venus");
ds_list_add(example_list,"Pluto");
```

This adds these strings to the ds list, in the preceding order.

Note   You can add multiple elements in one line of code, for example: ds_list_
add(example_list,"Earth","Mars","Jupiter,"Venus", "Pluto");

[YES I KNOW PLUTO IS NO LONGER A PLANET]
You could visualize this as

Index	Value
0	"Earth"
1	"Mars"
2	"Jupiter"
3	"Venus"
4	"Pluto"

Note   Like other data structures in GameMaker, the first index is 0, so a list with
5 values would have the locations of 0 through 4.

Sorting an Array

You can sort the list:

```
ds_list_sort(example_list,true);
```

This sorts elements in the list alphabetically.
Using false would organize it in reverse order.
Organized in order would then look like:

Index	Value
0	"Earth"
1	"Jupiter"
2	"Mars"
3	"Pluto"
4	"Venus"

Removing a Value

You can remove a value, for example, get rid of "Pluto" because it is not a planet:

ds_list_delete(example_list,3);

would remove the value of index 3 (namely "Pluto").

The ds list would then respond by moving other values up, so the list will then look like:

Index	Value
0	"Earth"
1	"Jupiter"
2	"Mars"
3	"Venus"

Index value

Adding a Value

A new element can be inserted:

ds_list_insert(example_list,1,"Neptune");

inserts new data at position 1.

Elements that follow will be moved down, so the list would then look like this:

Index	Value
0	"Earth"
1	"Neptune"
2	"Jupiter"
3	"Mars"
4	"Venus"

After adding an element you may want to sort your list again.

You can find where (if present) an element value is positioned:

```
position=ds_list_find_index(example_list,"Mars");
```

which would set the value of position as 3.

You can get the value of an element at a given location:

```
chosen=ds_list_find_value(example_list,4);
```

sets the variable to what is held at position 4.

A very useful bit of code allows you to get a value using the | accessor, so instead of the preceding code, you can obtain the value held directly. For example, an alternative to the preceding line of code could simply be written as:

```
chosen=example_list[| 4];
```

You may need to find the size of a list, for example:

```
list_size=ds_list_size(example_list);
```

sets the variable to the list size, see the following note.

Note   As a list starts it's reference 0, a list with four elements would return as four (there are contents at positions 0, 1, 2, and 3.

A list can be shuffled into a random order (great for card games):

```
ds_list_shuffle(example_list);
```

randomly shuffles the list.

It is important to get rid of the list when you have finished with it, this helps prevent memory issues:

```
ds_list_destroy(example_list);
```

removes the given ds list from memory.

Basic Projects

A)   Make a system that can hold five variables. If player presses X, allow them to add a new variable at the bottom of the list, and remove the top item. Draw this data onscreen.

B)   Populate a list with five fruits. Player to enter a guess of a fruit. If this is in the list, remove it and tell the player. When all have been guessed, the player wins.

C)   Make a system that draws the names of all students in your class in alphabetical order.

Advanced Project

D)   Populate a list with playing cards (use a loop for this), that is, AS for ace of spades, 5D for the five of diamonds. Shuffle this list, and deal out top five cards (and remove from the list) into 4 players' hands. Draw the players' hands onscreen.

Useful Functions

```
ds_list_clear()
ds_list_read()
ds_list_write()
```

allows for saving and loading data

Summary

You're now able to create a data structure, add, remove, and sort elements. You should now be able to identify when a ds list should be an appropriate data structure to use.

CHAPTER 23

Paths

Paths can be used make an instance move around in a pre-determined way. This can be useful for

- Making an enemy follow a patrol path.
- Graphical effects.
- Making a bomb or missile follow a curved path.

Path Example

Create a new path, path_example. Click four points, and select Smooth Curve and Closed, as shown in Figure 23-1.

© Ben Tyers 2023

B. Tyers, *GameMaker Fundamentals*, https://doi.org/10.1007/978-1-4842-8713-2_23

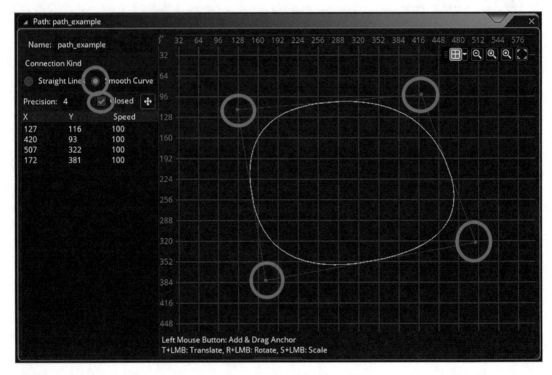

Figure 23-1. *Shows a basic path, set as smooth and closed*

Creating a Path in Code

The path editor is great for laying out your paths, but at times, you may want to do this in code. You can create a path and add points using code:

```
/// @description Make path
path_example_2=path_add();
path_set_closed(path_example_2, true);//sets as closed
path_set_kind(path_example_2,true);//sets as Smooth Curve
path_add_point(path_example_2,10,10,5);
path_add_point(path_example_2,100,10,5);
path_add_point(path_example_2,100,100,5);
path_add_point(path_example_2,10,100,5);
```

which creates a circular path

Make an object **obj_example**, and assign a sprite to it, setting the origin as center. Put the following in the **Create Event:**

```
/// @description Make a path with code
path_example_3=path_add();
path_set_closed(path_example_3, true);//sets as closed
path_set_kind(path_example_3,true);//sets as Smooth Curve
path_add_point(path_example_3,100,100,5);
path_add_point(path_example_3,300,100,5);
path_add_point(path_example_3,300,500,5);
path_add_point(path_example_3,550,450,5);
path_start(path_example_3,50,path_action_restart,true);
```

starts the given path at a speed of 50, and restarts when the end is reached, at an absolute position.

The path action sets what happens when the end of a path is reached. The options available are:

```
path_action_stop
path_action_restart
path_action_continue
path_action_reverse
```

Note   The final `true` value for `path_start` says to use absolute room coordinates (the same as the path), whereas `false` would base the path on the instances starting position.

Some useful functions you can use with paths.

You can insert a point:

```
path_insert_point(path_example,2,90,90,4);
```

inserting a new point at position 2.

You can change a point's location, or speed using the following, which would change the path's point at position 4 to an x and y of 75 with a speed of 5. This value is a percentage of the path speed, for example, 50 would be 50%.

```
path_change_point(path_example,4,75,75,5);
```

You can get the position of a point on a path:

```
xpoint=path_get_point_x(path_example,3);
ypoint=path_get_point_y(path_example,3);
```

allows you to store some path point.

The precision of curves can be assigned 1(low) to 8(high):

```
path_set_precision(path_example,4);
```

Drawing a Path

For testing purposes, you put the following in a Draw Event to draw the path:

```
/// @description Draw self and path
draw_self();
draw_path(path_example,x,y,true);
```

draws the path onscreen. Useful for a lot of purposes, especially when testing and debugging.

direction holds the value in degrees of the path is following at any given point.

This can be used with image_angle to make the instance point in the direction it is moving.

For example, pop the following in a Step Event of the current example:

```
/// @description Point direction moving
image_angle=direction;
```

Say, for example, you had a room set up like that shown in Figure 23-2, which has a maze and an enemy.

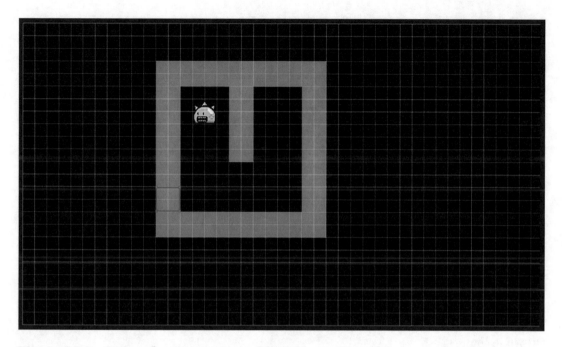

Figure 23-2. *Example room set up with maze and enemy*

With such a setup, you may want the enemy to patrol that area, create a new path path_example_4, so your resources tree looks like that shown in Figure 23-3.

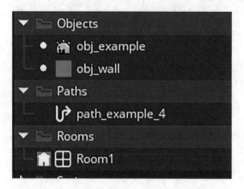

Figure 23-3. *Showing assets*

Open up the room and create a new **Path Layer**, as shown in Figure 23-4.

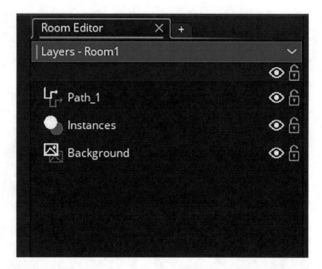

Figure 23-4. *With path added*

Next, select that layer and assign the path you created, and place four points, as shown in Figure 23-5.

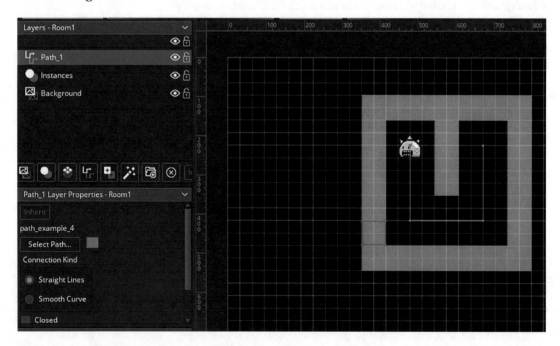

Figure 23-5. *Path assigned and points added*

Pop the following in the **Create Event** of **obj_example** and test.

```
path_start(path_example_4,50,path_action_reverse,true);
```

Basic Projects

A) Set an object to move in a circular path, on loop.

B) Allow mouse clicks to add points to a path, draw this path on screen.

Advanced Projects

C) Set a path for an object. Set the object's sprite to point the direction it is moving.

D) Make a system that sets ten random path points and save them to an ini file.

Useful Functions

You can make a path reverse from its current point:

```
path_reverse(path_example);
```

You can remove all points from a path:

```
path_clear_points(path_example);
```

You can create instances along a path with:

```
p=0;
n=500; // change to match how many trees to place evenly along the path
repeat (n)
{
    xx = path_get_x(path_example, p);
    yy = path_get_y(path_example, p);
    instance_create_layer(xx, yy, "Instances", obj_tree);
    p += 1/n;
}
```

Summary

You should now be able to set up a path using the path editor, and also in code. You can start a path and tell it what to do when the end of a path is reached. You understand the difference between absolute and relative paths.

CHAPTER 24

Functions

Using functions for code that is used often within your game is great way to make it easier to read and quicker to update. Additionally, it makes it easier to organize and understand how your code works. A GML function is also useful in processing data, especially if you will be doing the same calculation again and again. This can include sending data to the script, processing it, and returning an outcome or variable. If you are using the same code twice or more anywhere in your program, then you should consider using a function. This allows you to make just one change to update your code everywhere. Imagine a game that had over 100 enemy monsters with their own code; changing the code for each would take many hours and be prone to errors. Using a function, you could do this in a few minutes. It also allows for nice and tidy code. A function also allows you to easily share code between different game projects (which is a must if you go on to a career in game making) – saving you potentially a lot of time.

Some examples for scripts:

- Doing a math calculation and returning the answer, even if only used once; it means that your code is easier to read through and understand

- Setting a drawing or font type, formatting, and color – makes code easier to read, and quicker to set

- Playing sound effects and voices – you can send through which asset to play. For example, to play a music track and stop any music already playing

- Sending through an object and returning the closest instance – great for complex weapon systems

- Drawing code that's used multiple times – allowing you to quickly update it

- Recording bullet hits against multiple different objects

© Ben Tyers 2023
B. Tyers, *GameMaker Fundamentals*, https://doi.org/10.1007/978-1-4842-8713-2_24

- Adding things to a DS list

- Find if there is a clear path between two points

- Taking in a set of numbers and returning the average

- Any other GML that's used more than once

A function needs to be declared before you can use it. There are a few choices when declaring it, I use the following method.

A function is basically a container that includes one or functions. Then, generally return a result, for example a variable, a resource name, true false, etc.

It's good practice to give your function an appropriate name, so when you're calling it is clear as to what it does.

Creating a Function

First create a function in Scripts assets, as shown in Figure 24-1.

Figure 24-1. *Creating a new function*

You can then name the function and pop in some code, for example the following:

```
/// @function        get_total(value1,value2,value3)
/// @param {real}    real
/// @param {real}    real
/// @param {real}    real
function get_total(value1,value2,value3)
{
    var total=value1+value2+value3
    return total;
}
```

which returns a total of all three values.

This would look like that shown in Figure 24-2.

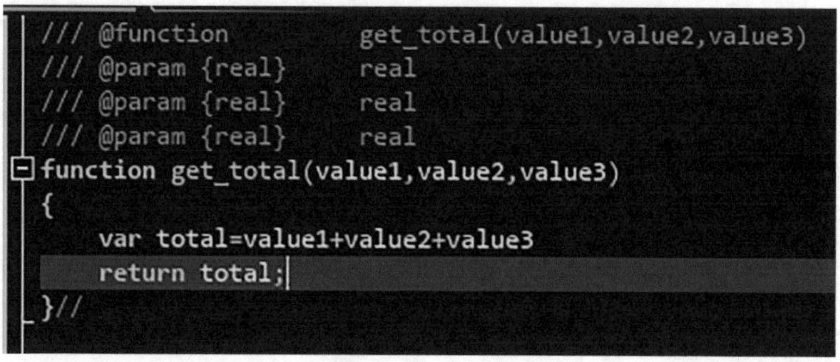

Figure 24-2. *Showing function added*

Calling a Function

You could call this function with the following:

```
get_total=function_example(10,12,40);
```

Then do something with the value, for example:

```
draw_text(100,100,get_total);
```

You can for example send through the ids of two instances function_check_y:

```
/// @function function_check_y(value1,value2)
/// @param {real} instance 1
```

```
/// @param {real} instance 2
function function_check_y(inst_1,inst_2)
{
    if (instance_exists(inst_1) && instance_exists(inst_2))
    {
        if inst_1.y < inst_2.y
        {
            return true;
        }
    }
    return noone;
}
```

This will return true if the first instance of the first instance is higher up on the screen than the second instance, returning false if not. No one will be returned if either or both don't exist.

Using return will return the given value and exit the script at that point, without processing any following code.

A script does not have to return a value, it can just be used to make something happen, for example, you could set it to make an effect over two given ids:

```
/// @function function_effect()
function function_effect(inst_1,inst_2)
{
    effect_create_above(ef_spark,inst_1.x,inst_1.y, 1,c_yellow);
    effect_create_above(ef_spark,inst_2.x,inst_2.y, 1,c_yellow);
}
```

Basic Projects

Create a script to do each of the following, and display any result onscreen visually as required, remembering to set up any text drawing style and alignment.

A) Take in five numbers and return the average value (rounded).

B) Check whether a player is within a certain distance of another object instance. Return true or false.

C) Takes in text and a position. Draws onscreen with a shadow.

Advanced Projects

D) A script that draws an effect at the midway point of two given object instances.

E) Takes in two object instances and draws the angle between, as if on a compass, that is, North or West.

Useful Functions

You can also set up a function that will tell you what the given variable needs to be.

For example:

```
/// @function function_example(value1,value2,value3)
/// @param {real} value1
/// @param {real} value2
/// @param {real} value3
function function_example(value1,value2,value3)
{
        total=value1+value2+value3
        return total;
}
```

Then when typing function_example in an **Event**, you'll see a reminder at the bottom, as shown in Figure 24-3.

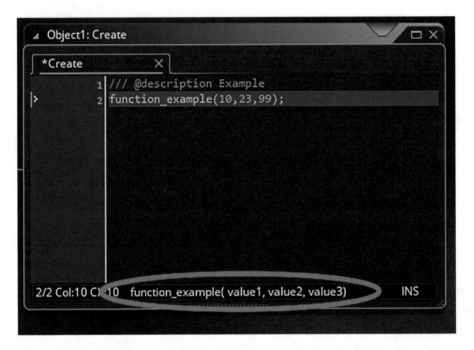

Figure 24-3. *Showing function information*

You can also set it to use a default value if an argument is not passed to the script, for example:

```
function draw_text_shadow(xx,yy,text,col=c_red)
{
    draw_set_font(font_text);
    draw_set_colour(col);
    draw_text(xx-2,yy-2,text);
    draw_set_colour(c_white);
    draw_text(xx,yy,text);
}
```

So the following would draw the text with a green shadow:

```
draw_text_shadow(200,200,"Example Text",c_green);
```

whereas this would draw a shadow with a red shadow:

```
draw_text_shadow(200,200,"Example Text");
```

Summary

You should now understand how to set up a script, when it should be used, and how to pass arguments to it. You now know how to test if something returns as true or false and make things happen based on that outcome.

CHAPTER 25

Tilesets

Tilesets are a light-weight way of adding graphics to your game, as opposed to using just objects. They can be used for such things as:

- Background elements
- Mazes
- Quick level creation

Setting a Tileset

Tilesets make use of sprites, so let's go ahead and load one in, as shown in Figure 25-1.

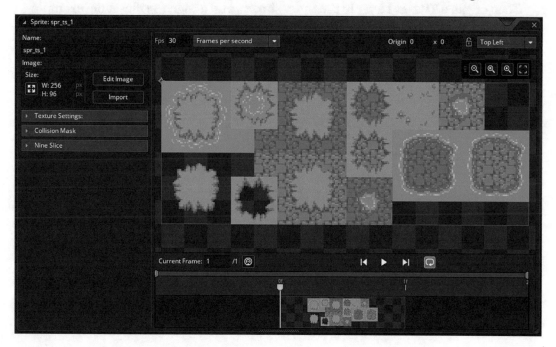

Figure 25-1. *Adding in a sprite for use as a tileset*

© Ben Tyers 2023
B. Tyers, *GameMaker Fundamentals*, https://doi.org/10.1007/978-1-4842-8713-2_25

Note   It should be noted that tileset sprites can only be **one** frame. All the components for the tileset are in a grid layout. You then use a part (or parts) to make your background in the room editor.

Next create a new tileset and assign this sprite and the appropriate settings, as shown in Figure 25-2.

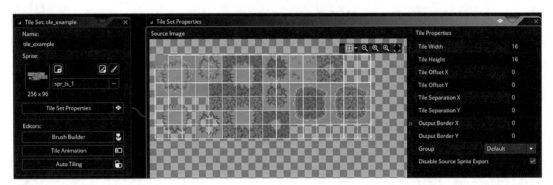

Figure 25-2. *Setting a tileset*

Then create a **Tileset Layer** in the order shown, and assign the tileset tile example you created, as shown in Figure 25-3.

Figure 25-3. *Setting a tile layer*

Placing Tiles

You can now select a sub-tile, by clicking the right, for example, as shown in Figure 25-4.

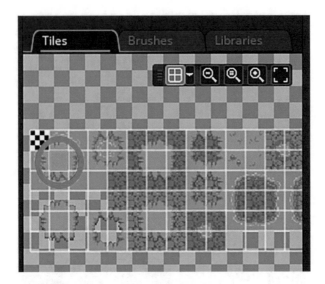

Figure 25-4. *Selecting a tile*

You can now paint this selected tile onto the room layer, by clicking in the room to build up your level, for example, as shown in Figure 25-5.

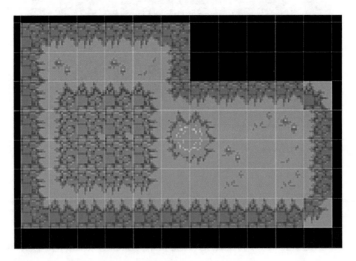

Figure 25-5. *Showing a tileset example*

Basic Project

A)   Use the RPG tileset and create a level layout.

Advanced Projects

B) Create a background setup using Cobblestone tileset, create an additional layer and place trees over it.

Useful Functions

```c
tilemap_set();
tilemap_get_at_pixel()
```

These functions allow for setting a tile so that can be used to dynamically change your tiles as the game is running.

Summary

You now know how to load in a sprite and set it for use as a tileset and use it create a level layout.

CHAPTER 26

Timelines

Timelines are a great way to make something happen in a predefined order and at a certain time. You can set it up to execute any code you wish, hence you can make a multitude of actions happen when you wish. As the set up uses only a single asset, editing and changing it can be done quickly. You could use a timeline to

- Spawn enemies at set times.

- Create a sequence of effects.

- Spawn health packs.

- Fire a spread of bullets.

Creating a Timeline

You can create a Timeline in the same way you would any other asset, as shown in Figure 26-1.

© Ben Tyers 2023

B. Tyers, *GameMaker Fundamentals*, https://doi.org/10.1007/978-1-4842-8713-2_26

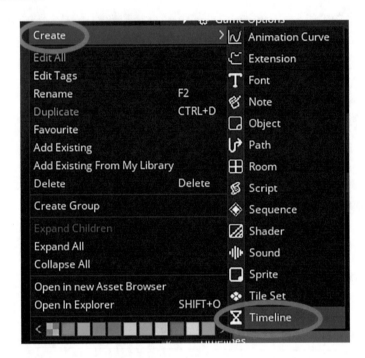

Figure 26-1. *Creating a timeline*

You can then name your timeline, as shown in Figure 26-2.

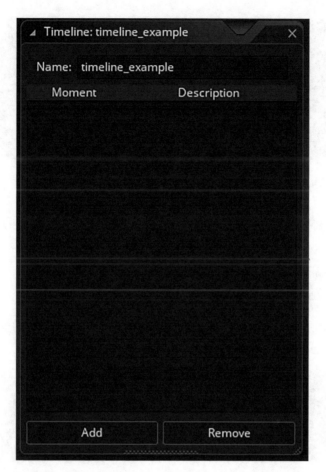

Figure 26-2. *Naming your timeline*

You can now click **Add** to create what is known as **Moment**. Click **Add** and edit the Moment to 60, as shown in Figure 26-3. This value tells the program when it should execute the code. At a default game speed of 60, this code would execute after one second, a value of 600 would be run at 10 seconds.

Figure 26-3. *Showing a moment added*

You can then put code into the moment, just as you would with any code, for example:

```
/// @description Create a firework
effect_create_above(ef_firework,room_width/2,room_height/2,5,c_red);
```

which after one second would create a firework in the middle of the room.

Your Timeline would then look like that shown in Figure 26-4.

Figure 26-4. *Showing code added to a moment*

You can also add/create other moments in the same way, for example, as shown in Figure 26-5.

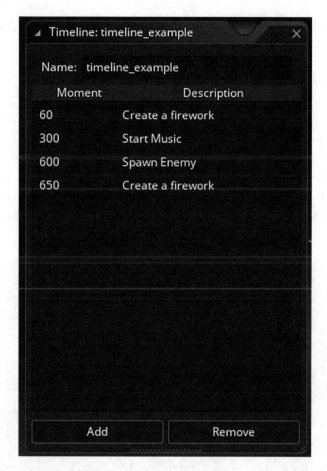

Figure 26-5. *Showing additional moments added*

Make a Timeline Play

You can make the timeline start by using

```
/// @description Start timeline
timeline_index = timeline_example;
timeline_position = 0;
timeline_running = true;
timeline_loop=true;
```

which would start the timeline and repeat until told otherwise.

189

The final line of the previous code can be changed to the following, so it plays through just once:

```
timeline_loop=false;
```

where setting:

```
timeline_running = false;
```

would stop the timeline.

If you have it on an endless loop and require a pause, you can add a moment like that shown in Figure 26-6, which will force the timeline to wait until that moment before looping:

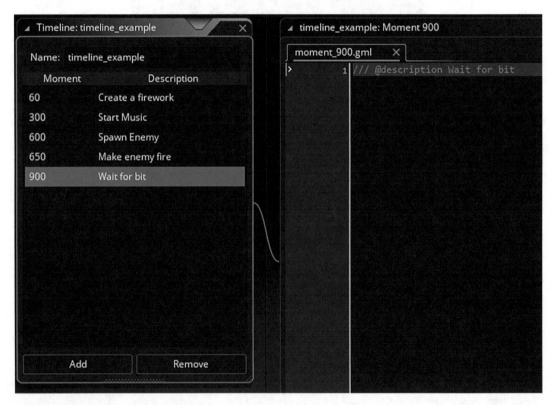

Figure 26-6. *Creating a moment to allow a short pause*

Basic Projects

A) Create a firework display using effects. Add audio that plays so it matches the effect. Make the display loop through five times and then stop.

Advanced Projects

B) Make an enemy patrol in a square pattern, shoot a melee of bullets each time it changes direction.

Useful Functions

You can create a timeline with:

```
example=timeline_add();
```

which would set the timeline to execute the given script after two seconds. You'll also find these useful:

```
timeline_size()
timeline_max_moment()
timeline_moment_add_script()
```

Summary

You now know how to make things happen at certain times in an orderly pattern.

CHAPTER 27

Views

There are times when you will want a larger play area than the window itself. Views can be used for this. Game genres that may require this are

- Space shooter.

- Racing game.

- Platformer.

Views can be set up using room settings or GML.

First let's set up a player **obj_player** and **obj_wall** with sprites assigned to them, resized to 64x64 with the origin as middle center. In the **Step Event** of **obj_player** pop in:

```
if keyboard_check(ord("A")) {x-=2;}
if keyboard_check(ord("D")) {x+=2;}
if keyboard_check(ord("W")) {y-=2;}
if keyboard_check(ord("S")) {y+=2;}
if x<0 x=0;
if x>room_width x=room_width;
if y<0 y=0;
if y>room_height y=room_height;
```

movement code for testing

Also create an object **obj_splash** with the following code in the **Create Event**. You do this because the starting room tells the game what the window size is (in this case 800 by 400), failure to do this may have undesired effects:

```
/// @description Goto room
room_goto(room_view_example);
```

Rename the room you have as **room_splash** and pop in an instance of **obj_splash**, setting the room size, as shown in Figure 27-1.

© Ben Tyers 2023
B. Tyers, *GameMaker Fundamentals*, https://doi.org/10.1007/978-1-4842-8713-2_27

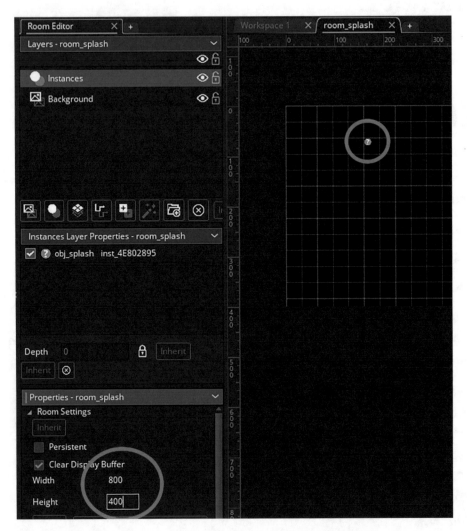

Figure 27-1. *Showing room settings and instance placed in room*

Setting a View

Next create a room **room_view_example** and set it as shown in Figures 27-2 and 27-3.

Figure 27-2. *Showing settings*

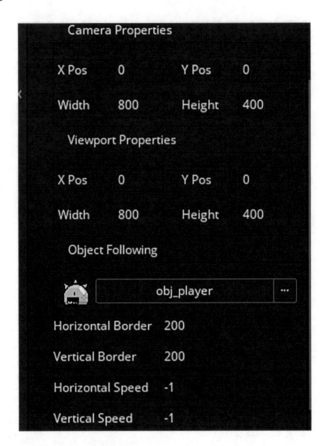

Figure 27-3. *Showing more settings*

Next, place one instance of **obj_player** in the room, and several of **obj_wall,** something similar to Figure 27-4.

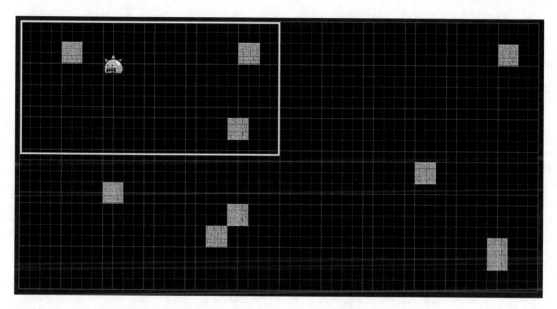

Figure 27-4. *Showing instances placed in room for testing*

Also note, in Figure 27-4, the white border that shows the view size.

Now test your game. If you've done everything correctly so far, you'll be able to move the player around. The view should show just a portion of the whole room, and move to follow the player.

It is also possible to set up and control views.

An example for this project is in the resources folder, named Chapter 27 – A.

If you have a view set up, you can reference it, for example, with

```
vcam=view_get_camera(0);
```

You can set the size with:

```
camera_set_view_size(vcam,400,400);
```

You can set it to follow an instance:

```
camera_set_view_pos(vcam,obj_example.x-100,obj_example.y-100);
```

Advance Projects

A) Make a split screen with two windows, each of which follows a separate instance.

B) Make a function that keeps two instances in view, adapting view as required.

Useful Functions

Sometimes it's useful to know the size, which can be done with:

```
width = camera_get_view_width(view_camera[0]);
height = camera_get_view_height(view_camera[0]);
```

There may be times you want to rotate a view, this can be achieved with:

```
camera_set_view_angle(view_camera[0], 45);
```

Summary

You now know how to set up a basic view that can follow an instance and keep it in view. You'll now be able to create larger play areas for your games.

CHAPTER 28

MP Grids

MP Grids allow you to create dynamic paths on the fly that will find a path between two points, avoiding instances along the way.

Great for

- Enemies searching for the player.
- Automated instances that search for food or supplies.

Setting a Grid

First you can set the grid size, depending on how your room is set up, for example:

```
global.grid=mp_grid_create(0,0,room_width / 64, room_height / 64, 64, 64);
```

which would set a grid size of 64.

You can set which instances need to be avoided by adding them to the grid:

```
mp_grid_add_instances(global.grid,obj_wall,true);
```

Adding Objects to a Grid

Adds obj_wall to be avoided.

You can then make the path between (you will first have to create a path resources prior to the following line):

```
mp_grid_path(global.grid,path,x,y,mouse_x,mouse_y,false);
```

Makes a path. The final true/false allows you to set whether the path can use diagonal movement. false is no diagonal, true would allow diagonals.

© Ben Tyers 2023
B. Tyers, *GameMaker Fundamentals*, https://doi.org/10.1007/978-1-4842-8713-2_28

Then start the path as you would any other path:

```
path_start(path,4,path_action_stop,true)
```

Let's start by creating an **obj_wall** with a wall sprite assigned and **obj_player** with a sprite assigned, resize both to 64x64 with origin as center.

Create a room and drop a few instances of **obj_wall** in it and one of **obj_player**, like that shown in Figure 28-1.

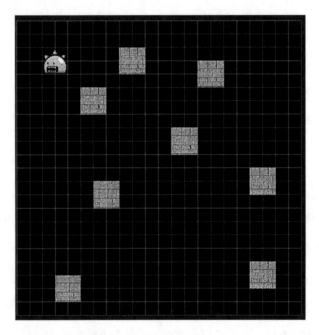

Figure 28-1. *Showing demo example room set up*

In **obj_player Create Event** put:

```
/// @description Setup
path=path_add();
global.grid = mp_grid_create(0, 0, room_width / 64, room_height / 64, 64, 64);
mp_grid_add_instances(grid, obj_wall, true);
```

sets up a path to use for path finding

In a **Draw Event** put:

```
/// @description draw self & path
draw_self();
draw_path(path,x,y,true);
```

This will draw the assigned sprite and path (if it has points on it).

And in a **Global Left Mouse Pressed Event** place:

```
/// @description Make a new path to mouse click location
path_clear_points(path);
mp_grid_path(global.grid, path, x, y, mouse_x, mouse_y, false);
path_start(path,4,path_action_stop,true);
```

If clicked on an empty area, will create a path to that point, avoiding any **obj_wall** and start the path.

mp_grid_path can also return a true or false value, depending on whether a valid path can be found.

For example:

```
valid=mp_grid_path(global.grid,path,x,y,mouse_x,mouse_y,false);
```

which would set valid to true or false

Basic Project

A) Make a setup as shown as follows. Make the instance move to and collect the gem. Upon collecting the gem, make the gem spawn in a free place and make a new path to it. As shown in Figure 28-A.

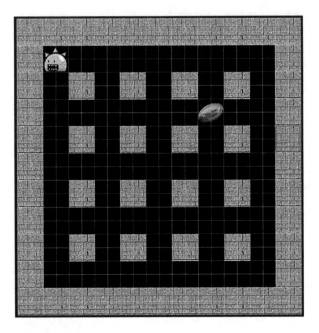

Figure 28-A. *Showing room setup*

Advance Project

B)   Make a room like that shown in the following. It has a start and end square. Make an instance move from start to end squares. Allow placing of walls by the player, only if it doesn't block a path to the exit, make an instance that must avoid the walls, and update its path as needed. As shown in Figure 28-B.

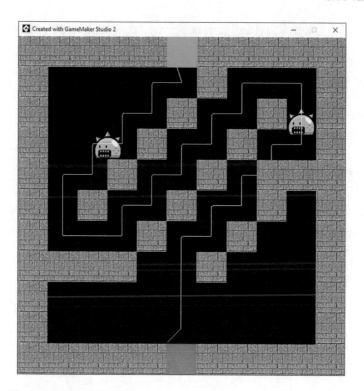

Figure 28-B. *Showing pathfinding*

Useful Functions

The following draws the grid using green and red, allowing you to see which "cells" have been marked off, great for testing and debugging, pop the following in a **Draw Event**:

```
draw_set_alpha(0.5);
mp_grid_draw(global.grid);
draw_set_alpha(1);
```

You can remove a marked cell from the grid, with, for example:

```
mp_grid_clear_cell(global.grid,4,5);
```

You can also add a single cell with:

```
mp_grid_add_cell(global.grid,2,3);
```

203

You can check an individual cell and check whether it has been marked or not, for example:

```
check=mp_grid_get_cell(global.grid,2,7);
```

which would be either `true` or `false`

Summary

You should now know how to set up a grid, add and remove cells, and create and start a path between two co-ordinates.

CHAPTER 29

Sequences

Sequences allow you to program in a set sequence that can be applied to one or more assets. It can play sounds, move objects, and move and animate sprites. Generally, you'll program this within the sequence editor rather than using GML.

Sequences are ideal for such things as:

- Moving buttons in for a menu

- Creating an effect, for example, when an enemy dies

- Animated cut-scenes

- Making a sprite rotate, like when collecting a bonus

- A boss level enemy movement and attack sequence

- Make a complex animation, like a swinging chain/rope

- Firing an intricate bullet spread

- Applying audio and graphical effects when a player collects an invincibility bonus

- Playing several sound effects in a set order

Let's start by creating a few assets that you'll use in the example.

Load in a bird sprite **spr_bird** – there is no object for this, as shown in Figure 29-1, resizing to 192x137. Also set the origin as middle center:

© Ben Tyers 2023
B. Tyers, *GameMaker Fundamentals*, https://doi.org/10.1007/978-1-4842-8713-2_29

Figure 29-1. *Showing spr_bird setup*

Next create a sound **snd_bird**, and load in a bird sound from the folder From **YoYo Games**.

Note   We won't be using left room editor tab for a bit, so you can click the X to close, so you have more space available for setting up your sequence. (Just click a Layout in the top bar, then Reset Layout, and then click any room in the asset tree to get this back.)

Creating a Sequence

Now create a new sequence, and name it **sq_example**, it will look like that shown in Figure 29-2.

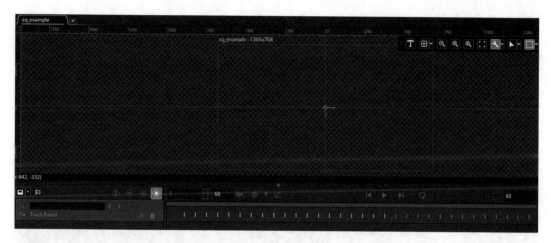

Figure 29-2. *Showing a blank sequence*

First thing you need to do is change the length of the sequence. It is currently set at a length of **60** (which at 60 steps per second is one second). Change to **300** (five seconds), as shown in Figure 29-3.

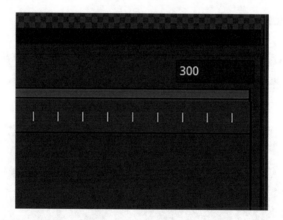

Figure 29-3. *Setting a length for the sequence*

Let's jump straight in and add an asset. Click and drag the bird sprite from the assets into the location shown in Figure 29-4, you'll notice that it is the left bottom of the gray square (this square represents a default room size, so placing here would mean the sequence starts in the bottom left of a room when we add it in later – if you are using a different room size, you can adjust this in the Preferences):

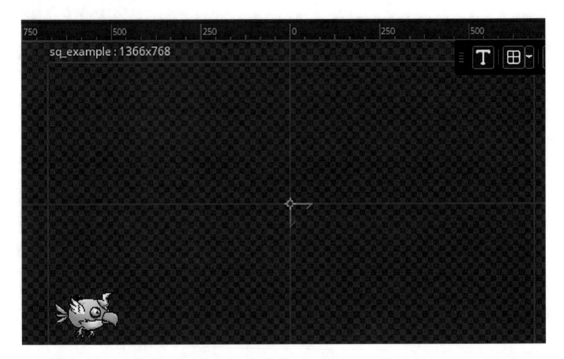

Figure 29-4. *Showing a sprite placed in the sequence*

In the bottom part of the screen, you'll see this sprite referenced on the tracking panel, as shown in Figure 29-5. This area will show any sprites, objects, sounds, etc. that you have added.

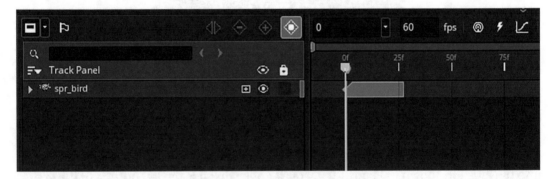

Figure 29-5. *Showing an asset added to the sequence*

In the middle section you'll see an orange bar, this tells the sequence how long the asset is to be present in the sequence. It's currently on a short period, so click and drag where shown in Figure 29-6.

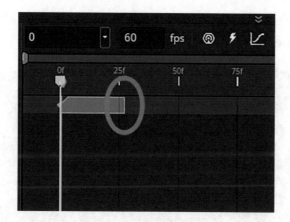

Figure 29-6. *Where to click and drag to extra time present*

Click and drag up to the end of sequence, level with the red line as shown in Figure 29-7. This ensures that the asset will remain viewable and present for the whole sequence.

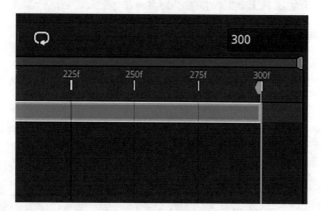

Figure 29-7. *Showing asset time set for whole sequence*

You now want to move the time to the end of the sequence; there are a few methods for doing this, like clicking where the numbers are above the orange bar (as in Figure 29-8).

I prefer to enter a number into the time box. So enter 300 in the box as shown to go to the end of the sequence, as shown in Figure 29-8.

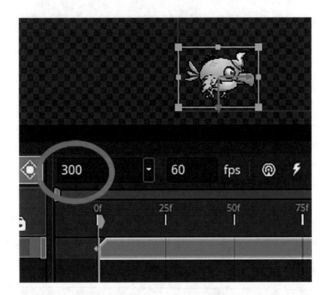

Figure 29-8. *Showing how to move to time in the sequence*

Now we'll drag the sprite of the bird to the far right of the gray box, as shown in figure 29-9.

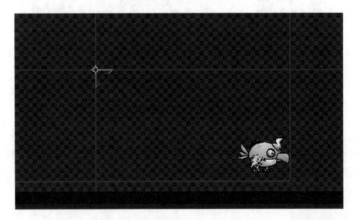

Figure 29-9. *Showing bird in bottom right for sequence time 300*

GameMaker will do all the animation needed to start this sprite at the bottom left for time position 0 and move it to the bottom right for time position 300. Press spacebar now and you'll see it move.

Let's set up to move up to the top middle of the gray box at the midway point (time 150).

So enter 150 in the box as before, and drag the bird to the top middle, as shown in Figure 29-10.

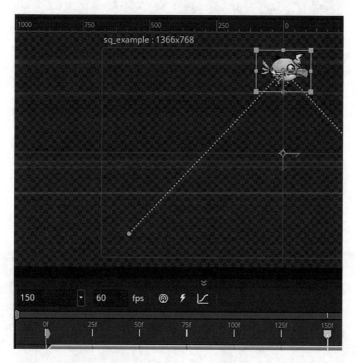

Figure 29-10. *Showing a new position for the sprite as time 150*

You can now press spacebar again to test.

Let's make it more interesting by changing the scale of the image as it moves.

Click where shown in Figure 29-11 to get some options to pop up:

Figure 29-11. *Showing where to click to select an option*

Setting a Scale Curve

Select the **Scale** option, as indicated in Figure 29-12.

Figure 29-12. *Showing where to find scale option*

Click **Scale** then **Convert To Curve**, as shown in Figure 29-13.

Figure 29-13. *Setting up for curve for changing scale*

Now again enter 150 in the box to go to the middle of the sequence, then click where shown to drag up so the curve looks like that shown in Figure 29-14.

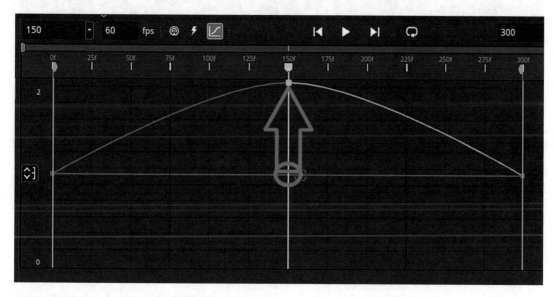

Figure 29-14. *Dragging up to form a curve*

This blue curve represents the **X** scale (think of it like image_xscale), you'll also want to do this for the **Y** scale. Click as indicated in Figure 29-15 to select the **Y** scale:

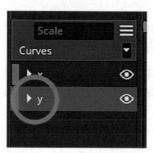

Figure 29-15. *Selecting y scale*

Make the curve the same as you did previously. When done, both curves should match up like that shown in Figure 29-16.

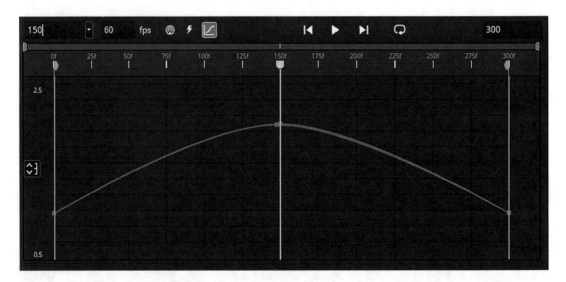

Figure 29-16. *Showing x and y scales matching*

You can now test by pressing spacebar again.

You can also add audio to a sequence, go to position 150 again by typing it in the time box.

First click in an empty area of the main window, so nothing is selected, then drag over the sound asset you created at the start of this chapter into the main sequence window.

It will now play this sound when the bird reaches the middle of its sequence – being both at the top middle and largest scale.

Presently, your sequence is set up to play once through, you can also set it up to repeat, or play and reverse continually. You can set this by clicking where shown in Figure 29-17.

Figure 29-17. *Setting loop type*

Note   Setting the loop type not only applies to the sequence preview, it also applies to the sequence when you use it in your game.

To add a sequence to a room, one method is to create a new Asset Layer and give it a name, for example, as shown in Figure 29-18.

Figure 29-18. *Making a layer for putting your asset on*

You can now drag your sequence from the resources tree onto this layer.

Note   To make positioning your sequence easier, you may want to turn off snapping to position, as shown in Figure 29-19.

Figure 29-19. *Turning off snap to make positioning of sequence easier*

An example for this project is in the download resources.

You also add in objects and make them move around in preset sequences, in a similar fashion to moving sprites.

Basic Project

A)   Make eight stars that start at the center of the room and move outwards and out the room, make the stars increase in size as they do this.

Advance Project

B)   Make an animated skeleton move from the left to the right, jumping over static boxes as it does so. Play a jumping sound each time it jumps and stop the skeleton's animation while it is jumping.

Useful Functions

```
layer_sequence_create()
layer_sequence_destroy()
```

Otherwise, I won't be providing any functions for Sequences as it is beyond the scope of this book – covering just the basics would require a whole book on its own.

Even with just the basics you've learnt in this chapter, you'll be able to create some pretty awesome effects, cool animations, cutscenes, and more.

Summary

You should now have a basic grasp of Sequences and have an idea of how capable they can be.

We've only covered the basics, but sequences are a very capable tool, so feel free to look more into what it has to offer.

APPENDIX A

Game – Plane Game

We'll now put into practice everything you've learnt to make a small fun shooting game. This game will include

- Parallax Background

- Music and Audio Control

- A Highscore Save System Using INI Files

- A HUD with Score, Healthbar and Lives

- Enemy Spawning System Using Alarms and Timelines

- Health and Lives System

- Paths for Enemies

- Functions for Processing Data

- Multiple Room Layers

- An Interactive Menu System

- Fonts and Text Management

- Enemy AI That Targets The Player

- DS Lists for Randomizing Enemy Spawning

- Randomization for Generating Background Items

- Collectible Items

- Paths for Enemies to Follow

- Effects When Hit or Collecting Items

- Various Rooms for Different Game Elements

- Lots of Collisions for Player, Enemies, and Projectiles

© Ben Tyers 2023
B. Tyers, *GameMaker Fundamentals*, https://doi.org/10.1007/978-1-4842-8713-2

- Mouse and Keyboard Input

- Health, Lives, and Score Management

- Sprite Control and Drawing

- A Weapon Control System

- Lots of Conditional Structures for Game Control

- Script for choosing an enemy

- Various Variables to Keep Track of What's Going On Within the Game

In this game, you control a plane through an endless level. You will shoot the enemies and avoid their weapons. There are four enemy types, each of which behaves differently, with separate ways to move and attack the player. The game will have a basic parallax background to give the illusion of movement. The aim is to get the highest score and survive as long as possible, and to collect bonuses for health, lives, extra points, and weapons. Player loses health if hit by an enemy or enemy's weapons. The game will have a splash screen to set up the game and load any current highscore. The menu will allow you to start the game, view game info, or exit to windows. In addition, there will be a "gameover" screen displaying the player's final score, and updating the saved highscore if a new record is achieved.

I'll show all steps required to make this game. I have omitted most of the downloading and sourcing of audio and graphics as that is not really within the scope of this book, though I included importing and setting up/formatting of images. All assets used are available in the download that comes with this book. There is also a completed project file that you can import.

I'll be using the Rubber Duck technique when making this game. This method assumes you are explaining how to do something to a rubber duck – so every detail is explained. See www.freecodecamp.org/news/rubber-duck-debugging/ for a more in-depth explanation. Feel free to skip over sections that you are comfortable with.

When I start a new project, I generally do things in the following order:

1. Plan out main game features with a pen and paper.

2. Source suitable graphics and audio – checking the license for each, ensuring that I can use it for the project.

3. Set up splash screen room.

4. Set up Menu room.

5.   Set up Game Information room.

6.   Set up Gameover room.

7.   Set up first level (which could be just 1 or many depending on the game).

8.   Create HUD.

9.   Create Main Player.

10.   Create Player Weapons.

11.   Create Bonuses.

12.   Create Enemies.

13.   Create Enemy Weapons.

14.   Create Enemy Spawning System.

15.   Create Effects.

Note   This shows the final code I have settled on; for most of the programming, I have written the code, tested, rinsed, and repeated until I get GML that works as I want it to. Sometimes this can take a lot of time, on a simple game like this one, the code is not so complex; for more complex games, expect to spend a few hours tweaking just one block of code.

Plan Out Main Game Features with a Pen and Paper

Although making and programming a game can be a dynamic process, I generally sketch out the look of a game on paper, make notes on what objects there will be and how they interact with each other. Sometimes this can be just a page or two, or more – a recent project had over 30 pages of notes stuck on my floor. For a simple game like this, it is just one page, plus the notes I made at the start of this chapter. This does a great job of explaining what this game entails.

> **Note**   The preceding is known collectively as a design document. This is very common in the gaming industry. Large teams may work on the design of a game for months before starting to make it.

A lot of the time you'll add a feature, think of better option and program this instead. Creating a game is a creative process, and I personally welcome adding new ideas while working on a game project.

Source-Suitable Graphics and Audio

As mentioned previously, I won't include sourcing most of the images, just the formatting, which will be covered in the following sections.

All the assets used in this game are in the resource download folder **Game**.

Let's head over to FlamingText.com and create a suitable logo for the game, as shown in Figure A-1, so add shadows or edit in an image editor to add effects, etc., if you so choose.

Figure A-1. *An example logo*

Import this into a new GameMaker project, and name the sprite as **spr_logo** and set the origin as middle center.

We'll use this sprite on the splash screen, menu, game info, and gameover rooms.

Note   Just because you find a resource (sprites, images, sound effects, music, etc.) on the Internet does not mean it is ok for you to use it in your game. I recommend that for each and every asset that you do not make yourself or pay someone, you check the licensing terms on the website. You may be able to use it, for example under Creative Commons, or if the source website says you must give credit – then give credit. If the website says you cannot use it, then don't use it! Creative people can spend a lot of time creating the assets, you cannot just go ahead and use them. Some creators or websites take copyright infringement very seriously, so you could get sued. If you look at the start of the book, every asset source I use has been provided. This is not intended as legal advice.

Set Up Splash Screen Room

First rename the default room name as **room_splash**, this will be the first room that is run.

Let's create a background for it. Create a new sprite **bg_menu** and load in the sprite from the resources folder, **splash_and_menu_background**. You'll notice that the image is particularly large, so let's resize so it can fit into the splash room. There is a quick shortcut for doing this – click where shown in Figure A-2.

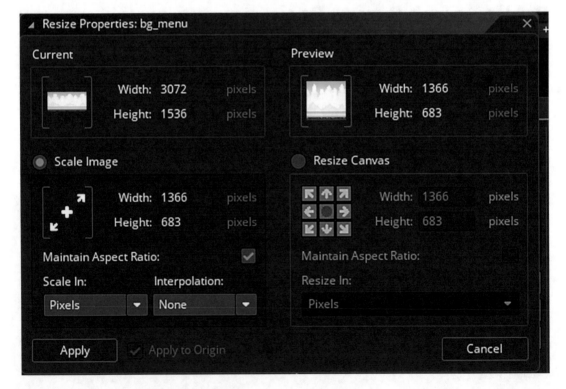

Figure A-2. *Quick method for resizing an image*

Set the dimensions as shown in Figure A-3, clicking Apply to set the changes.

Figure A-3. *Setting new image size*

Set this sprite as the background for **room_splash**, checking the box for stretch so the image fills the whole room, as shown in Figure A-4.

Figure A-4. *Setting background image and stretch option*

Next we'll set up an object that will be used to initialize the variables needed for the game.

Create an object **obj_splash** and assign the sprite **spr_logo** to it. Pop the initialization code into its **Create Event**:

```
/// @description Set up
//position in middle of room
x=room_width/2;
y=room_height/2;
```

```
alarm[0]= game_get_speed(gamespeed_fps)4;//show splash screen for 4 seconds
//Create ds list for enemy spawning
global.enemy_list=ds_list_create();
score=0;//declare starting score
health=100;//declare starting health
lives=5;//declare starting lives
global.special_weapon=5;//start with 5 special weapons
global.shots_fired=0;// so you can keep track of shots fired
global.hits=0;// so you can keep track how many hits player makes
global.kills=0;//to keep track of player's kills
//load any highscore - set as 0 if no data
ini_open("gamedata.ini");
global.highscore = ini_read_real("data", "highscore", 0);
ini_close();
```

Then put the following into an **Alarm 0 Event**:

```
/// @description Go to menu
room_goto(room_menu);
```

Place an instance of this object into **room_splash**, as shown in Figure A-5.

Figure A-5. *Showing room with instance added*

That is all for this room.

Set Up Menu Room

First, create a new font **font_button** and set as Arial size 20. We'll use this font to draw descriptions on the menu buttons.

Next we'll source some buttons you can use for the menu, so head over to clickminded.com/button-generator/ to create some sprites.

Let's make some nice big buttons, in three different colors, for example, blue, green, and red as shown in Figure A-6.

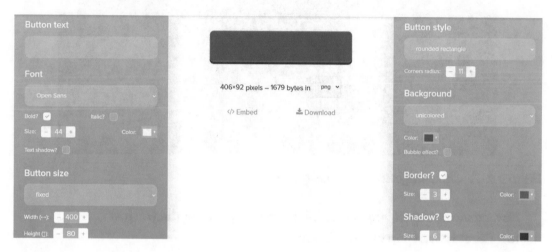

Figure A-6. *Showing a button set up*

Once you've downloaded them, create a sprite **spr_button** and import all three images and set the origin as middle center, and order them as shown in Figure A-7. Setting the origin as middle center will make it easier to position them in the middle of the room, and also make formatting the text to appear centered when you assign it to draw later.

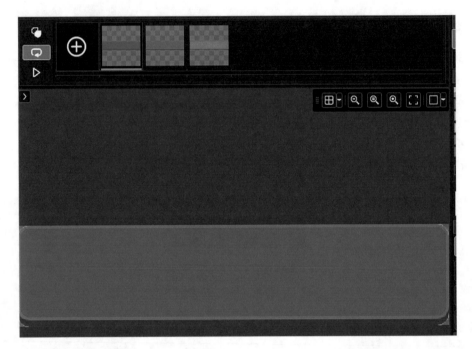

Figure A-7. *Showing button sprites added*

Now create an object, **obj_menu_play,** and assign the sprite you just created.
In a **Create Event** pop in the following:

```
/// @description Set up
image_speed=0;//turn off animation
image_index=0;//set initial image
display="PLAY GAME";
///move to middle
x=room_width/2;
```

We'll use the **Step Event** to control the button with:

```
/// @description Control Sprite && Detect Click
//change subimage on mouse over button (or not)
if position_meeting(mouse_x,mouse_y,id)
{
     image_index=1;
}
```

```
else
{
     image_index=0;
}

//change image if left button pushed on it:
if position_meeting(mouse_x,mouse_y,id) && mouse_check_button(mb_left)
{
     image_index=2;
}

//Do something on mouse release over button
if position_meeting(mouse_x,mouse_y,id) && mouse_check_button_
released(mb_left)
{
     room_goto(room_game);
}
```

We'll draw the button and assigned text with the following in the **Draw Event**:

```
/// @description Draw Button & Text
draw_self();//draw currently assigned subimage
draw_set_font(font_button);
//set allignment
draw_set_halign(fa_center);
draw_set_valign(fa_middle);
draw_set_colour(c_white);//set text colour
draw_text(x,y,display);
```

Next we'll set up two other buttons, first is **obj_menu_info** with the **Create Event** code set as

```
/// @description Set up
image_speed=0;//turn off animation
image_inde=0;//set initial image
display="GAME INFO";
///move to middle
x=room_width/2;
```

and it's **Step Event** code as

```
/// @description Control Sprite && Detect Click
//change subimage on mouse over button (or not)
if position_meeting(mouse_x,mouse_y,id)
{
     image_index=1;
}
else
{
     image_index=0;
}

//change image if left button pushed on it:
if position_meeting(mouse_x,mouse_y,id) && mouse_check_button(mb_left)
{
     image_index=2;
}

//Do something on mouse release over button
if position_meeting(mouse_x,mouse_y,id) && mouse_check_button_
released(mb_left)
{
     room_goto(room_info);
}
```

The **Draw Event** code is the same, with

```
/// @description Draw Button & Text
draw_self();//draw currently assigned subimage
draw_set_font(font_button);
//set allignment
draw_set_halign(fa_center);
draw_set_valign(fa_middle);
draw_set_colour(c_white);//set text colour
draw_text(x,y,display);
```

and a final button to exit to Windows with the **Create Event** code:

```
/// @description Set up
image_speed=0;//turn off animation
image_inde=0;//set initial image
display="QUIT GAME";
///move to middle
x=room_width/2;
```

Step Event with

```
/// @description Control Sprite && Detect Click
//change subimage on mouse over button (or not)
if position_meeting(mouse_x,mouse_y,id)
{
     image_index=1;
}
else
{
     image_index=0;
}

//change image if left button pushed on it:
if position_meeting(mouse_x,mouse_y,id) && mouse_check_button(mb_left)
{
     image_index=2;
}

//Do something on mouse release over button
if position_meeting(mouse_x,mouse_y,id) && mouse_check_button_
released(mb_left)
{
     game_end();
}
```

and the **Draw Event** with the same as previously used:

```
/// @description Draw Button & Text
draw_self();//draw currently assigned subimage
draw_set_font(font_button);
```

```
//set allignment
draw_set_halign(fa_center);
draw_set_valign(fa_middle);
draw_set_colour(c_white);//set text colour
draw_text(x,y,display);
```

Now load in the music we'll use for the menu, **snd_music_menu**, which is in the resources folder. We'll set up as shown in Figure A-8, this option reduces the overall size of your game, and is the ideal setting for music in most cases.

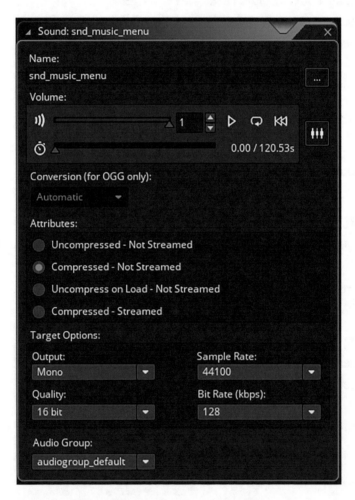

Figure A-8. *Showing audio settings for menu music*

Next create a new object, **obj_menu_logo** and assign **spr_logo** to it. Pop the following in its **Create Event**:

```
/// @description Music Control
audio_stop_all();//stop anything already playing
audio_play_sound(snd_music_menu,1,true);//play music on loop
```

Create a new room, **room_menu** and apply the same background as for the splash room, remembering the **Stretch** option for the background. Add one of each of the button objects and one of **obj_menu_logo**, as shown in Figure A-9.

Figure A-9. *Showing menu set up*

Set Up Game Information Room

Next we'll create a room to display some information about the game. Create a room **room_info** and assign the same background as used previously.

Create a new font, **font_info**, let's use Comic Sans size 22, as shown in Figure A-10.

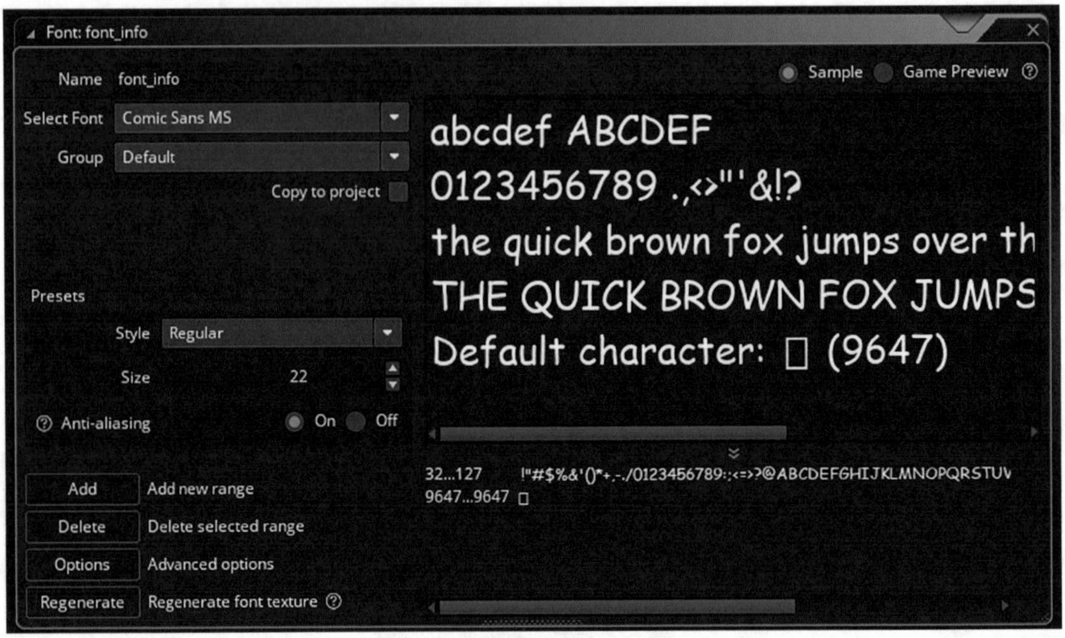

Figure A-10. *Showing font_info settings*

Create an object **obj_info** and assign **spr_logo**. You won't use default drawing, just assigning it so you can see it placed in room.

Pop the following in the **Create Event**:

```
/// @description Set alarm
alarm[0]=game_get_speed(gamespeed_fps)*5;
```

and in an **Alarm 0 Event**:

```
/// @description Back to menu
room_goto(room_menu);
```

and in a **Draw Event**:

```
/// @description Draw stuff
draw_sprite_ext(spr_logo,0,room_width/2,100,0.5,0.5,0,c_white,1);
draw_set_font(font_info);//set font
//set allignment
draw_set_halign(fa_center);
draw_set_valign(fa_middle);
draw_set_colour(c_black);//set text colour
```

```
draw_text(room_width/2,room_height/2,"Example Game\nMove With Keys W And D\
nShoot Bullet With Left Mouse Button\nShoot Special Weapon With Right Mouse
Button\n\nShoot Enemies\nAvoid Enemies & Bullets\n\nCollect Crates For More
Special Weapons");
```

When tested, this will look like that shown in Figure A-11.

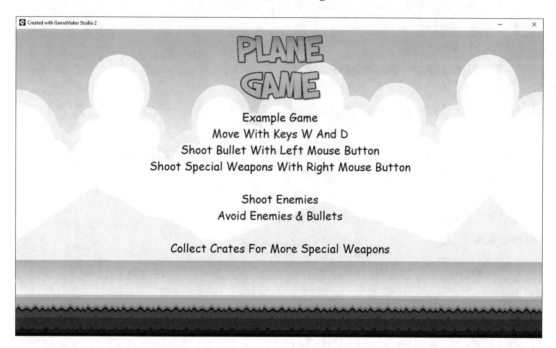

Figure A-11. *Showing game info room in action*

Set Up Gameover Room

Next we'll set the room that the player will go to when they have lost all their lives and
health. It will show some stats that the player has achieved, and also check whether the
player has set a new highscore. Create a room, **room_gameover** and set the background
as before, remembering to select the Stretch option in Background settings.

Create a new object **obj_gameover** and assign the sprite **spr_logo** to it.

In its **Create Event,** put the following code that checks whether the player has or
has not set a new highscore and update, if required. It will also set a string we'll use as a
message when you draw the player's statistics, we'll also center it in the room.

```
/// @description Check for highscore
if score>global.highscore//check if better than current highscore
{
      ///save to ini file if bigger
      ini_open("gamedata.ini");
      ini_write_real("data", "highscore", score);
      ini_close();
      //set a message
      score_message="New HighScore";
}
else//do this if not a new highscore
{
              score_message="No New HighScore - Best Score Was
              "+string(global.highscore);;
}
//center on screen
x=room_width/2;
```

In the **Step Event**, put the following code that will allow the player to restart the game:

```
/// @description Restart Game on Left Mouse Button Pressed
if mouse_check_button_pressed(mb_left)
{
      game_restart();//restart game
}
```

and in a **Draw Event**, put

```
/// @description Draw Logo & Game Data
draw_self();//draw assigned sprite
draw_set_font(font_info);//set font
//set allignment
draw_set_halign(fa_center);
draw_set_valign(fa_middle);
draw_set_colour(c_black);//set text colour
draw_text(x,450,"Your Score "+string(score));
```

```
draw_text(x,480,score_message);
draw_text(x,510,"Shots Fired "+string(global.shots_fired));
draw_text(x,540,"Shots Hit "+string(global.hits));
draw_text(x,570,"Kills "+string(global.kills));
draw_text(x,630,"Left Mouse Button To Restart");
```

You'll probably want to test that this all works as expected, but wondering how you could do this without an actual game to test yet. What I tend to do is create an object for testing with some random data. Create a new object **obj_testing** and put the following code in the **Step Event**:

```
/// @description For testing
if keyboard_check(ord("X"))
{
        score=irandom(1000);
        global.shots_fired=irandom(1000);
        global.hits=irandom(1000);
        global.kills=irandom(1000);
        room_goto(room_gameover);
}
```

Pop an instance of this object in **room_menu**. I usually put such instances in the top left of the room. It will appear as a grey circle, as shown in Figure A-12. This grey circle will not appear in game, it just shows in the IDE.

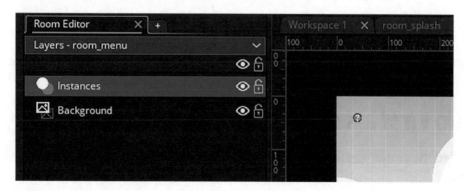

Figure A-12. *Adding instance for testing*

237

Before you go any further, let's tidy up the resources tree a bit. Create a new folder in the Objects section by right clicking with mouse and selecting Create Group, as shown in Figure A-13.

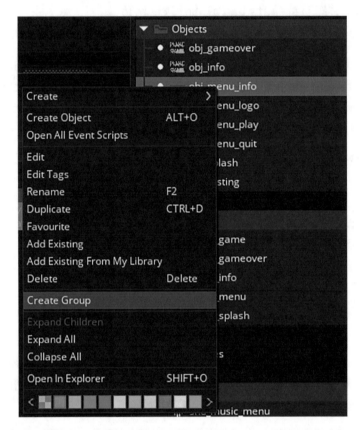

Figure A-13. *Creating a group for assets*

Name it as Menu. You can now select the objects and drag them into this folder.

Set Up First Level

Create a room, **room_game**. This will be the room where the main game action will take place.

First we'll make the background with the parallax effect. Load in the backgrounds, **bg_far** setting as a size of 1366x1104, **bg_sky** as 728x768, and **bg_near** as its current size of 518x136.

Create a background layer for each of **bg_far**, **bg_sky**, **bg_near** and an Instance Layer, as shown in Figure A-14.

Figure A-14. *Showing new layers added*

Set up layer **far** as shown in Figure A-15.

Figure A-15. *Showing far layer properties*

Set up sky layer as shown in Figure A-16, noting the Horizontal Speed of -2.

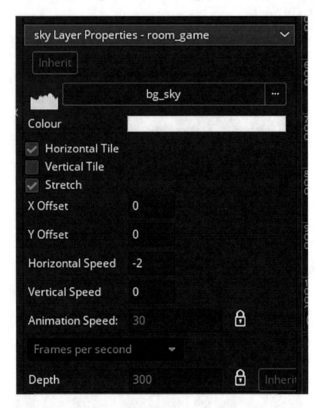

Figure A-16. *Showing sky layer settings*

For the **near** layer, set as shown in Figure A-17, again noting the Horizontal speed setting of -3.

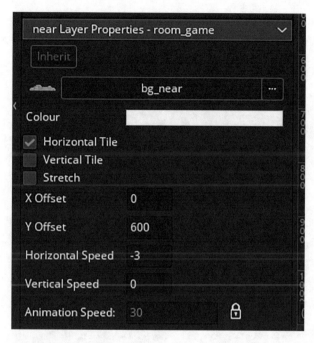

Figure A-17. *Properties for the near layer*

Create a sprite **spr_water** and import all the water subimages, as shown in Figure A-18.

Figure A-18. *Showing imported subimages*

Create an object, **obj_water** and assign this sprite to it. On the water Instances layer, place these objects along the bottom of the room, as shown in Figure A-19.

Figure A-19. *Showing background set up and instances obj_water added*

As a final stage we'll create some clouds that will move across the room, helping to break the otherwise boring background.

Create an object **obj_cloud** and load in the three cloud images to **spr_cloud**, changing the size to 220x107 and setting the origin as middle center, as shown in Figure A-20.

Figure A-20. *Assigning cloud sprite to an object*

Pop the following code in the Create Event:

```
/// @description Choose a random position, speed, and cloud
x=room_width+sprite_width;//create to the right of room
y=irandom_range(50,600);//choose a random y position in top part of
the room
hspeed=random_range(-5,-2);//choose a random speed to move left
image_speed=0;//prevent animation
image_index=irandom(2);//choose a random subimage
```

In a **Step Event**, put the following code. This will destroy the instance when the game is done with it.

```
/// @description detroy when off screen to the left
if x<0-sprite_width
{
        instance_destroy();
}
```

Note   Destroying instances when done with them helps free up memory, especially relevant with instances like this where you keep creating them – failure to do this will create a memory leak and eat up system resources, potentially crashing the game and the user's computer.

Create a new Instance Layer named **clouds**, in the position shown in Figure A-21.

Figure A-21.   *Showing new layer added*

Next we'll create an object that will spawn these clouds. Create an object **obj_spawn_clouds** and put the following in the **Create Event**:

```
/// @description Set initial alarm
alarm[0]=game_get_speed(gamespeed_fps);
```

and in an **Alarm 0 Event**:

```
/// @description Spawn cloud and restart the alarm
instance_create_layer(x,y,"clouds",obj_cloud);
alarm[0]=game_get_speed(gamespeed_fps)*random(4);
```

There is no sprite for this object. Pop an instance of this object in the top left of the game room, as shown in Figure A-22, upon the cloud layer.

Figure A-22. *Showing cloud-spawning instance placed in room*

Create HUD

Next we'll set up the HUD. We'll do this mainly through drawing code, but we'll use a sprite to show the number of lives that the player has.

Go ahead and load in a sprite from the Player Plane folder, naming as **spr_lives** and resize as shown in Figure A-23, also setting the origin as center so drawing it later is easier.

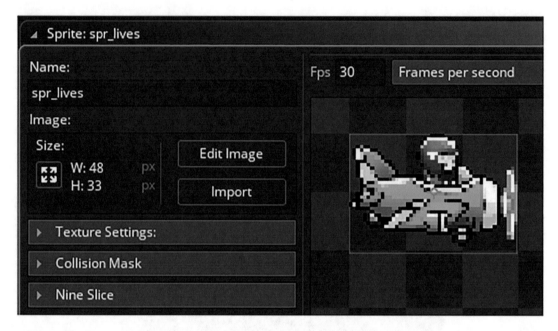

Figure A-23. *Setting sprite to be used for drawing player lives*

Also set up another sprite, spr_hud_special, as shown in Figure A-24.

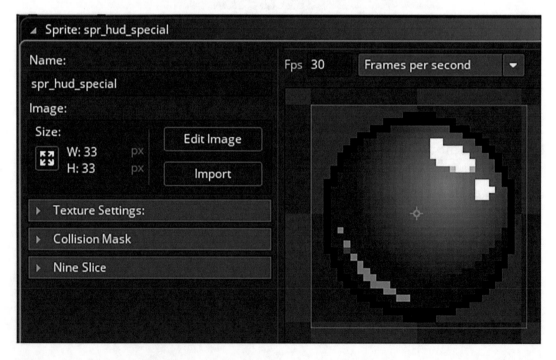

Figure A-24. *Setting sprite for use in HUD*

We'll also need a font to draw data, let's use something that's easy to read – Arial Black size 22 would work well. Set up a new font **font_hud** as shown in Figure A-25.

Figure A-25. *Setting a font for drawing the HUD*

Create an object, obj_HUD and put the following in the **Draw GUI Event**. Drawing in this event ensures that the HUD text and images will be drawn above everything else within the game.

```
/// @description Draw The HUD
///draw a border
draw_set_colour(c_white);
draw_roundrect(20,698,1346,748,true);
var middle=723;//this is the middle y position - will use to make code
                below easier
//draw lives as images
for (var pos=0;pos<lives;pos++)
{
    draw_sprite(spr_lives,0,1120+(pos*45),middle);
}
```

```
//draw special weapon as images
for (var pos=0;pos<global.special_weapon;pos++)
{
      draw_sprite(spr_hud_special,0,770+(pos*45),middle);
}
//draw the health bar
draw_healthbar(40,middle-20,400,middle+20,health,c_white,c_gray,
c_gray,0,true,true);
//Set Font and text settings
draw_set_font(font_info);//set font
draw_set_halign(fa_left);
draw_set_valign(fa_middle);
draw_set_colour(c_blue);//set text colour
//draw text
draw_text(980,middle,"LIVES:");
draw_text(610,middle,"SPECIAL:");
//format code with leading zeros
draw_text(410,middle,"SCORE: "+string_repeat("0",3-string_length(string
(score)))+string(score));
//Change font allignment
draw_set_halign(fa_center);
draw_text(220,middle,"HEALTH");
```

We'll also use this object to keep track of the player's lives and health, and take the player to the gameover room if they run out. We'll also add a few lines so you can reduce the health for testing purposes. Place the following code in a **Step Event**:

```
/// @description Control
if keyboard_check(vk_left)
{
      health--;
}

//Cap health
//reduce lives if out of health
if health<=0 && lives>=1
{
```

```
        lives--;
        health=100;
}
if health<0 and lives=0
{
        room_goto(room_gameover);
}
```

Now is a great place to save and test your game. You'll now be able to see the HUD and adjust your health.

Note   I didn't just magically type the code in previous draw event straight off. It took some time to adjust the positions of the text and the sprite sizes so it looks OK. This is all part of the design and coding process (and a fun part of programming) – don't get disheartened if you don't get the correct look for your game on the first try.

Create Main Player

As the room has been set up to give the illusion of moving to the left, all you need to do control-wise is move the player object up and down, and perhaps slightly change the image angle to make it look a bit better.

Next we'll set up the player object's main movement and assign a sprite. First create the sprite **spr_player**, which consists of two subimages. Resize to 192x131 and set the origin as center, as shown in Figure A-26.

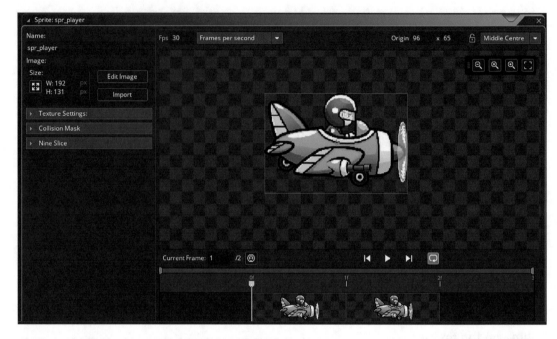

Figure A-26. *Setting up player's sprite*

Create an object, **obj_player** and assign this sprite.

In the **Create Event** pop the following:

```
/// @description Set Up
midpoint=275;//set middle and starting point
y=midpoint;//start player in middle
```

And in the **Step Event** place the code:

```
/// @description Movement control
if (keyboard_check(ord("W"))) {y-=2;}
if (keyboard_check(ord("S"))) {y+=2;}
y=clamp(y,50,600);//keep player in fixed range
//angle control
var angle=y-midpoint;//get difference
image_angle=0-(angle/20);//slightly angle plane
```

We'll come back to this event and add more code in the next section.

Create a new Instance Layer named player and put at the top in the room layers, as shown in Figure A-27, and place an instance of obj_player as shown. Now is a great point to save and test. You'll be able to move your player around, but won't be able to leave the room via the top or bottom.

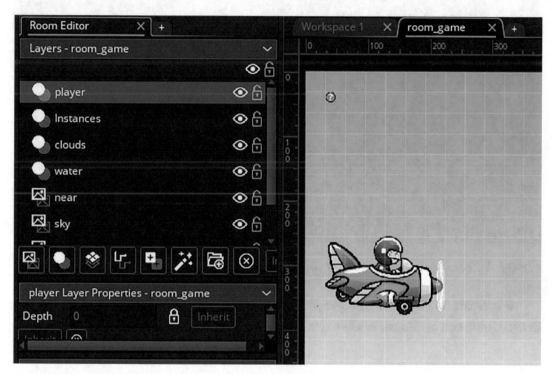

Figure A-27. Showing new layer added and instance of obj_player

Create Player Weapons

The player will have two type of weapons, a standard gun bullet that they can fire once every second, and a special weapon that can also fire once per second but the player has only a limited number available – though they can collect crates for extra ammo.

First we'll create the standard bullet. You don't need to resize this, but do set the origin as center. Create a sprite, **spr_player_bullet** as shown in Figure A-28.

Figure A-28. *Showing spr_player_bullet imported*

Next create an object **obj_player_bullet**, assign the sprite and add an Outside Room Event, which can be found, as shown in Figure A-29.

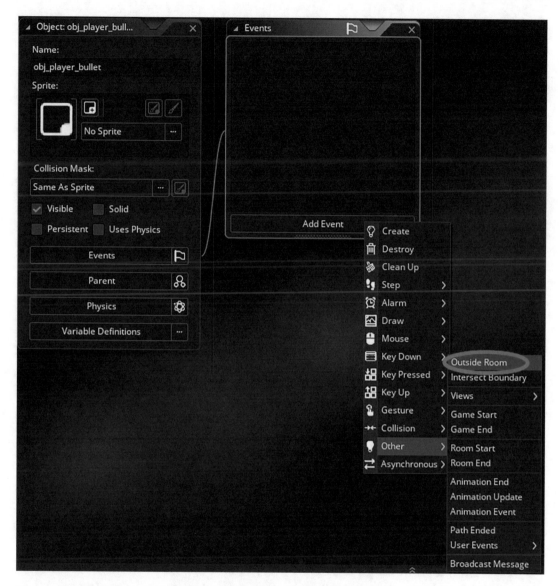

Figure A-29. *Showing location of outside room event*

Pop the following code into this event. This will destroy the instance when it's outside the room, helping to prevent a memory leak:

```
/// @description Destroy
instance_destroy();
```

That's all for this object.

Next create a new sprite **spr_player_special** and load in the sprite as shown in Figure A-30, resizing to 25x34 and setting the origin as center.

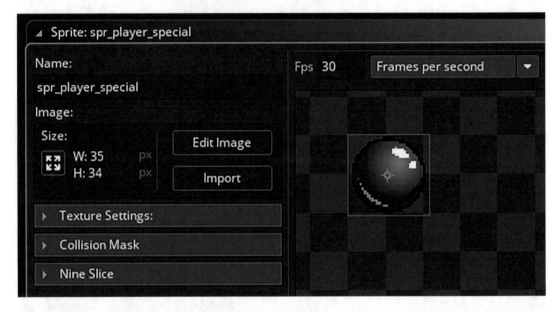

Figure A-30. *Setting up spr_player_special*

Create an object, **obj_player_special** and assign this sprite, and also make an **Outside Room** Event with the same code:

```
/// @description Destroy
instance_destroy();
```

That's both weapons set up.

Next we'll set the player up to shoot them.

Open up **obj_player**, and change the **Create Event** to that shown in the following. These additions add two flags that will be used to determine whether the player can shoot or not.

```
/// @description Set Up
midpoint=275;//set middle and starting point
y=midpoint;//start player in middle
can_shoot_bullet=true;//allow bullet shot
can_shoot_special=true;//allow special shot
```

Add an **Alarm 0 Event** with

```
/// @description Allow shooting bullet
can_shoot_bullet=true;
```

And an **Alarm 1 Event** with

```
can_shoot_special=true;//allow special shot
```

We'll use a new layer, **bullets** for spawning the bullets and special weapons, so create that now and order the layers as shown in Figure A-31.

Figure A-31. *Showing new bullets layer inserted*

Next we'll add a **Global Left Button Pressed Event** to **obj_player**, which can be found as shown in Figure A-32.

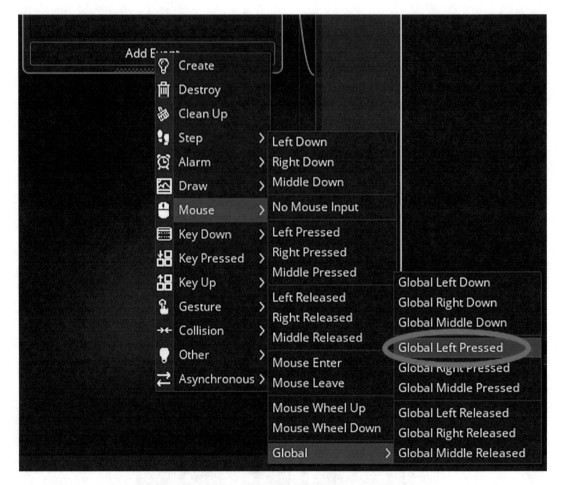

Figure A-32. *Showing where to find global left pressed event*

Pop the following code into this event:

```
/// @description Shooting bullet control
if can_shoot_bullet
{
    var bullet=instance_create_layer(x,y,"bullets",obj_player_bullet);
    //spawn the bullet
    bullet.speed=4;//set the speed of bullet
    bullet.direction=image_angle;//match direction to that of the plane
    bullet.image_angle=image_angle;//make the bullet point to direction
                                of movement
    can_shoot_bullet=false;
```

```
        alarm[0]=game_get_speed(gamespeed_fps);
    global.shots_fired++;//update shot count
}
```

The use of var in the preceding block tells GameMaker that it is a local variable and only needed for that specific block of code.

Next create a **Global Right Button Pressed Event** with the following code, which will check if the player can shoot, and check if there is ammo available. If available, it will spawn seven special bullets in a spread.

```
/// @description Special bullet control
if can_shoot_special && global.special_weapon>0
{
        global.special_weapon--;//reduce available weapons
        start_angle=-30;
        can_shoot_special=false;//set flag so cant shoot again
        alarm[1]=game_get_speed(gamespeed_fps);set alarm to allow
        shooting again
        repeat(7)
        {
                var bullet=instance_create_layer(x,y,"bullets",obj_player_
                special);//spawn the bullet
                bullet.speed=4;//set the speed of bullet
                bullet.direction=image_angle-start_angle;//match direction to
                                                that of the plane
                bullet.image_angle=image_angle-start_angle;//make the bullet
                                                point to direction
                                                of movement
                start_angle+=10;
                global.shots_fired++;//update shot count
        }
}
```

Also add a Key X Pressed Event and put the following code into it, which will readd the number of special weapons available – you can use this for testing:

```
/// @description testing
global.special_weapon=5;
```

Create Bonuses

In this game there is one bonus that will replenish the player's special weapon.

Create a new sprite **spr_bonus** and assign the sprite and set the origin as the center.

Create an object **obj_bonus** and assign this sprite, as shown in Figure A-33.

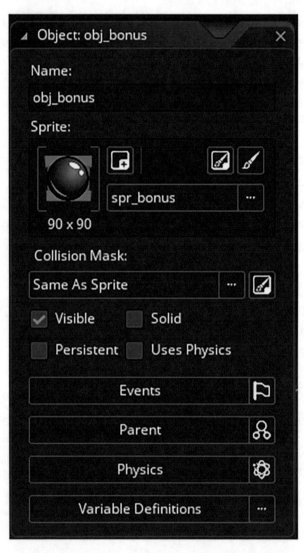

Figure A-33. *Obj_bonus with sprite spr_bonus assigned*

In a **Step Event** pop the following:

```
/// @description rotate
image_angle+=2;
//destroy if off left of screen
if x<0-sprite_width
{
        instance_destroy();
}
```

Next set up a **Collision Event with obj_player**, as shown in Figure A-34.

Figure A-34. *Collision event code when collecting a bonus*

Next, we'll make an object that spawns this item. Create an object **obj_spawn_bonus** and put the following in the Create Event:

```
/// @description Set an alarm
alarm[0]=game_get_speed(gamespeed_fps)*8;set for 8 seconds
```

and the following in the **Alarm 0 Event**. This will reset the alarm, and with a 1 in 4 chance will create a bonus instance:

```
/// @description Spawning control
alarm[0]= game_get_speed(gamespeed_fps)*8;//reset for 8 seconds
```

```
var select=irandom(3);//choose either 0 1 2 or 3
if select=0// has a 1 in 4 chance of happening
{
        varr xpos=room_width+sprite_width;//just off right of screen
        var ypos=irandom_range(50,600);//random y position - in a range that
                                    player can move to
        var bonus=instance_create_layer(xpos,ypos,"bullets",obj_bonus);
              bonus.hspeed=random_range(-8,-3);//set movement within a range
}
```

Pop an instance of this on the room's bullet layer, as shown in Figure A-35.

Figure A-35. *Showing spawning instance added*

Now is an ideal place to save and test your game. You'll now be able to move, shoot, and collect the bonus for more special weapons.

Create Enemies

We'll create three enemy types, each of which behaves in a slightly different manner with regards to movement and shooting of its weapons. We'll create a separate object for each enemy to keep it simple. The enemies will share a bullet object.

Note   Creating a separate instance for each enemy is a great starting method, though note that when you become more proficient you'll learn new ways of doing this.

First we'll set up the sprites. We'll use a different color sprite for each: red, orange, and blue.

Create a new sprite **spr_enemy_blue** and import the sprite. Resize to 192x167 and set the origin as Middle Center, as shown in Figure A-36.

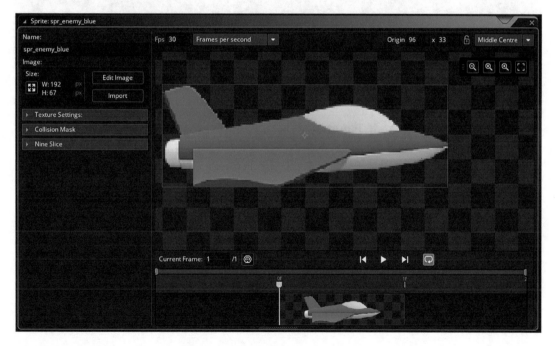

Figure A-36. *Showing resized sprite with origin set*

As the enemies will be coming from the right side of the screen, we'll need to have the plane pointing to the left. Click Edit Image as shown in Figure A-37.

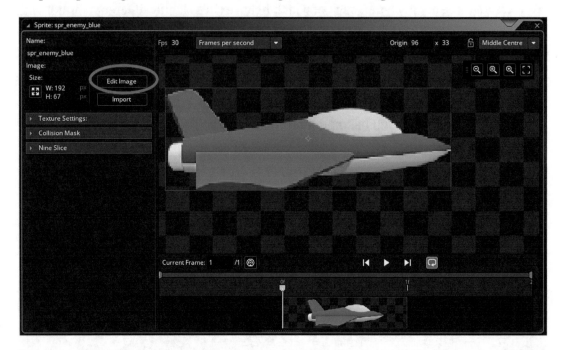

Figure A-37. *Showing where to click to edit image*

Next click where shown in Figure A-38 to mirror the image so it points to the left.

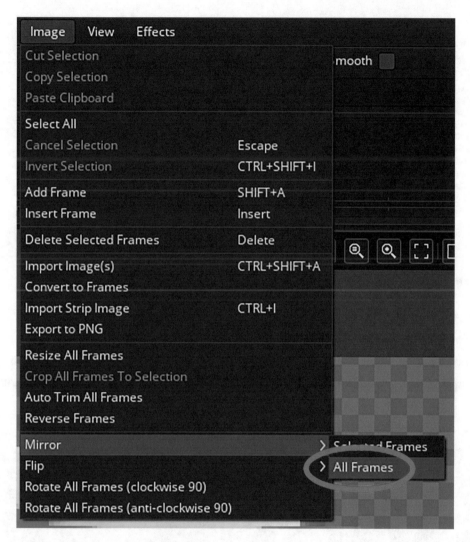

Figure A-38. *Mirror image to point to the left*

Next create new sprite **spr_enemy_red** and load in the subimages, as shown in Figure A-39.

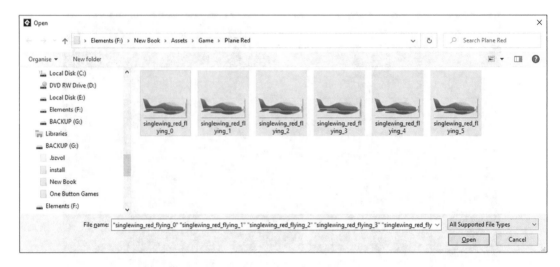

Figure A-39. *Loading in subimages for spr_enemy_red*

Resize as 192x83 and set the origin as center.

Also edit this image so it points to the left.

The final sprite is **spr_enemy_orange**. Import the subimages, resize as 192x80, set the origin as center and mirror the image to point to the left. When done, it will look like that in Figure A-40.

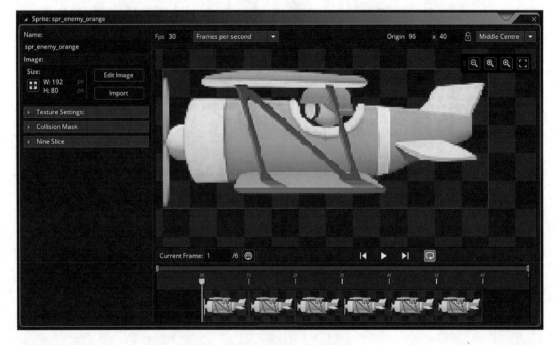

Figure A-40. *Showing sprite spr_enemy_orange setup*

Next we'll set up the bullet for the enemies, **obj_enemy_bullet**.

Create this object and assign a bullet sprite **spr_enemy_bullet**, as shown in Figure A-41, pointing to the right and origin as the center.

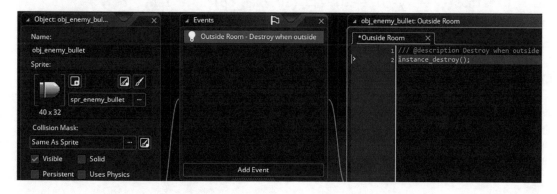

Figure A-41. *Showing enemy bullet sprite*

Make an object, **obj_enemy_bullet** and assign this sprite.

Make an Outside Room Event and put this code in:

```
/// @description Destroy when outside
instance_destroy();
```

as shown in Figure A-42.

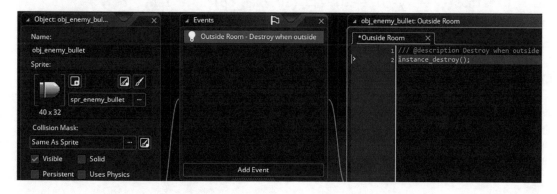

Figure A-42. *Showing outside room event*

We'll set the first enemy to move across the screen from the right to the left and shoot bullets straight across the room.

Create an object **obj_enemy_1** and assign the blue sprite **spr_enemy_1**.

In the **Create Event** put

```
/// @description Start alarm for shooting && set health
alarm[0]=game_get_speed(gamespeed_fps)*6;
hp=4;
max_hp=hp;
hspeed=-1;
```

In an **Alarm 0** Event, pop in the code in the next block. This will reset the alarm and spawn a bullet, setting the image angle and direction:

```
/// @description Create bullet and restart alarm
alarm[0]=game_get_speed(gamespeed_fps)*3;
//create bullet and set direction, image angle and speed
var bullet=instance_create_layer(x,y,"bullets",obj_enemy_bullet);
bullet.direction=180;
bullet.image_angle=180;
bullet.speed=3;
```

We'll also set up drawing a small healthbar above the instance so the player can see what hp the enemy has.

Make a **Draw Event** and put in the following:

```
/// @description Draw self & healthbar
draw_self();
draw_healthbar(x-30,y-50,x+30,y-30,(100/max_hp)*hp,c_red,c_red,
c_green,0,true,true);
```

We'll also add a Step Event to keep track of hp of the enemy and destroy it if it has run out. This can be done with

```
/// @description Check hp
if hp<=0 instance_destroy();
```

When done, this enemy will look like that shown in Figure A-43.

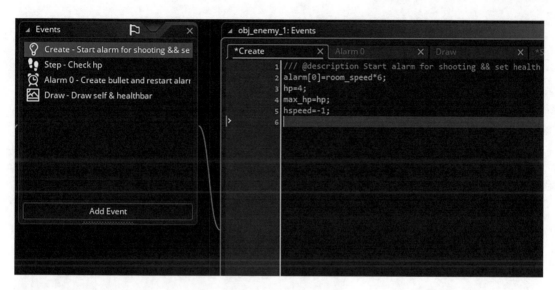

Figure A-43. *Showing obj_enemy_1 events set up*

Next create the second enemy, **obj_enemy_2,** which has the sprite **spr_enemy_red** assigned. We'll make this instance move into the room and then move up and down.

It has a **Create Event** with

```
/// @description Start alarm for shooting && set health && set up moving
alarm[0]=game_get_speed(gamespeed_fps)*6;
hp=3;
max_hp=hp;
hspeed=-3;
active=false;
```

and a **Step Event** with

```
/// @description HP & movement control
if hp<=0 instance_destroy();
//set as sctive if on screen at position
if x<1100 && active==false
{
     hspeed=0;
     vspeed=-3;
     active=true;
}
```

```
//move direction if reached top area
if active && y<100
{
      vspeed=3;
}
//move direction if reached bottom area
if active && y>600
{
      vspeed=-3;
}
```

And an **Alarm 0 Event** for spawning the bullet. This setup spawns the bullet that moves to the player's plane position – meaning they will have to dodge the bullet.

```
/// @description Create bullet and restart alarm
alarm[0]=game_get_speed(gamespeed_fps)*3;
//create bullet and set direction, image angle and speed
var bullet=instance_create_layer(x,y,"bullets",obj_enemy_bullet);
var dir=point_direction(x,y,obj_player.x,obj_player.y);
bullet.direction=dir;
bullet.image_angle=dir;
bullet.speed=3;Fixe
```

And finally, a **Draw Event** to draw the sprite and healthbar:

```
/// @description Draw self & healthbar
draw_self();
draw_healthbar(x-30,y-50,x+30,y-30,(100/max_hp)*hp,c_red,c_red,
c_green,0,true,true);
```

The third and final enemy plane will move in while following a path, move around a bit and then leave the window and then destroy itself.

Let's create a path **path_enemy_3**, as shown in Figure A-44.

Figure A-44. *Showing new path added*

Next create a new path layer in the room, you can name it enemy_path as shown in Figure A-45.

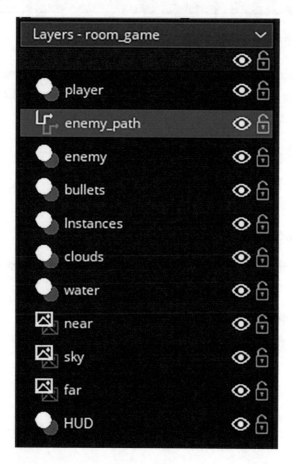

Figure A-45. *Showing new path layer added*

Next create a path that looks something like that shown in Figure A-46. Note, in the settings on the left, that the selected path is path_enemy_3 and set as a smooth curve.

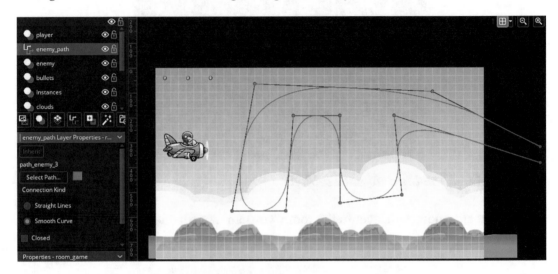

Figure A-46. *Showing created path and settings*

Next create the last enemy object, **obj_enemy_3** and set the sprite **spr_enemy_ orange**. In the **Create Event**, you set up the alarm for shooting, set the hp, and start on the path you just created.

```
/// @description Start alarm for shooting && set health
alarm[0]= game_get_speed(gamespeed_fps)*3;
hp=4;
max_hp=hp;
path_start(path_enemy_3,4,path_action_stop,true);
```

In a **Step Event**, put the following so the game destroys the instance when it runs out its health hp:

```
/// @description HP & movement control
if hp<=0 instance_destroy();
```

Make an **Alarm 0 Event** with the following code. This resets the alarm and creates a spread of bullets:

```
/// @description Create bullet and restart alarm
alarm[0]= game_get_speed(gamespeed_fps)5;
//create bullet and set direction, image angle and speed
var start_angle=-20;
repeat(5)
{
     Var bullet=instance_create_layer(x,y,"bullets",obj_enemy_bullet);
     //spawn the bullet
     bullet.speed=4;//set the speed of bullet
     bullet.direction=image_angle-start_angle+180;//match direction to
                                              that of the plane
     bullet.image_angle=image_angle-start_angle+180;//make the bullet
                                                  point to direction of
                                                  movement
     start_angle+=10;
}
```

We'll also add a **Path Ended Event**, which can be found, where shown in Figure A-47.

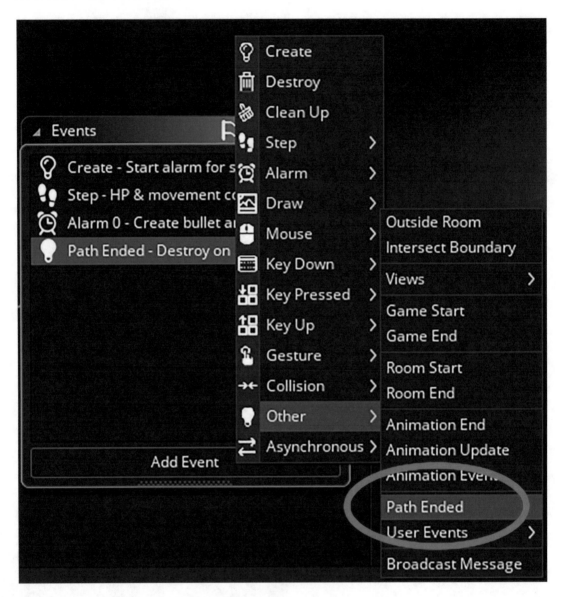

Figure A-47. *Adding a path ended event*

Pop the following code into this event:

```
/// @description Destroy on path end
instance_destroy();
```

As before, pop the following into a **Draw Event**:

```
/// @description Draw self & healthbar
draw_self();
draw_healthbar(x-30,y-50,x+30,y-30,(100/max_hp)*hp,c_red,c_red,
c_green,0,true,true);
```

Create Enemy Spawning System

You now require some kind of system to spawn the enemies.

This first thing that may come to mind is to use the choose function to select a random object to spawn, something like

```
to_spawn=choose(obj_enemy_1,obj_enemy_2,obj_enemy_3);
```

The problem with this approach is that it may not spawn instances in a balanced way, for example, there could five instances of **obj_enemy_1** spawned in succession.

Another method that we'll use is to use a ds_list to store the objects, shuffle the order, and pick the top value, making a note of it, removing it from the list, and then spawning that object. This keeps an even distribution of the planes.

To keep this tidy, we'll create a function that can be called. You'll see in the following that we get the current size of the list, and repopulate if empty, then it will make a selection. Add this function now, as shown in Figure A-48.

```
//Function spawn enemy
function spawn_enemy()
{
        //check size of current list
        //if empty repopulate with planes
        if ds_list_size(global.enemy_list)==0
        {
                repeat(6)
                {
                        //add to list
                        ds_list_add(global.enemy_list,obj_enemy_1,obj_
                        enemy_2,obj_enemy_3);
                }
```

```
        //mix them up so random order
        ds_list_shuffle(global.enemy_list);
}
///grab the top element
var to_spawn=global.enemy_list[|0];
//remove from list
ds_list_delete(global.enemy_list,0);
//spawn this enemy
plane=instance_create_layer(room_width+140,irandom_
range(50,600),"enemy",to_spawn);
}
```

Figure A-48. *Showing function added*

Next set up an object that will be used to call this function, **obj_spawn_enemy**. In a **Create Event**, put

```
/// @description Set initial alarm
alarm[0]= game_get_speed(gamespeed_fps);
```

and an **Alarm 0 Event** with

```
/// @description Call script and reset alarm
spawn_enemy();
alarm[0]= game_get_speed(gamespeed_fps)*5;
```

Pop an instance of this in the room, where shown in Figure A-49.

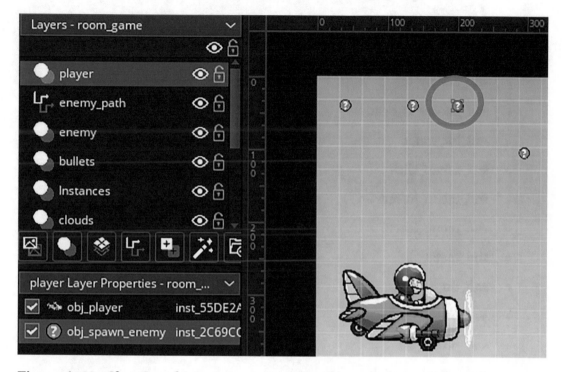

Figure A-49. *Showing obj_spawn_enemy placed in room*

Now is an ideal time to save and test your game. You'll now have enemies appearing that you can shoot at.

Collisions, Effects, and Audio

The next stage is to add some interaction between the objects, and do things like increasing the score, creating explosions and effects. I generally do this as the last thing in a game's creation, as I now know what all the objects are, what they do, and how they'll interact with each other.

First we'll set up some audio, create the sounds in the following list, choosing what you think is a suitable sound from the **Collection By SubSpaceAudio** sub folder and from the **YoYo Games** folder.

- snd_bonus_pick_up

- snd_enemy_bullet

- snd_enemy_bullet_big

- snd_enemy_hit

- snd_enemy_is_dead

- snd_hit_water

- snd_menu_click

- snd_menu_hover

- snd_menu_leave

- snd_metal

- snd_no_ammo

- snd_player_bullet

- snd_player_hit

- snd_player_special

We'll need one additional object that you'll use to create an effect when a bullet (player's or enemy's) hits the water.

Create an object **obj_water_effect** and assign a sprite **spr_water_effect** assigning the sprite subimages, as shown in Figure A-50, this time we'll set the origin as Bottom Center.

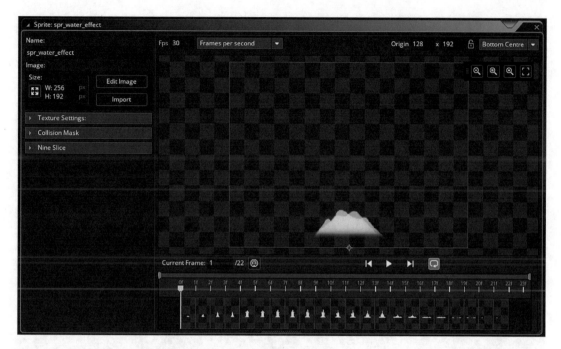

Figure A-50. *Showing spr_water_effect set up*

It has a Create Event with the following code. This makes it move to the left at the same speed as the **near** background layer. If you didn't do this, it would just look weird.

```
/// @description Start moving to match parallax effect
hspeed=-3;
```

It also has an **Animation End Event**, which can be found, as shown in Figure A-51.

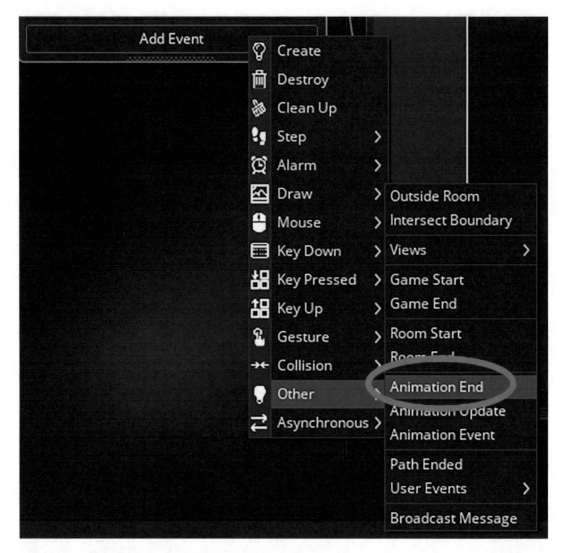

Figure A-51. *Showing animation end event*

Add the following block of code, which will destroy the instance once it has animated through all subimages once.

```
/// @description destroy
instance_destroy();
```

Let's now start adding in the sounds, effects, and collisions to the game.

We'll start by adding some audio interaction to the menu buttons.

Note   As we'll be doing exactly the same thing with all three menu buttons, we are going to use a Parent object to control the sound effects. This saves a lot of time, and also allows for editing how the buttons interact with the mouse very easily.

Create a new object, **obj_menu_parent**. It does not need a sprite assigned to. Make a **Mouse Enter Event**, as shown in Figure A-52.

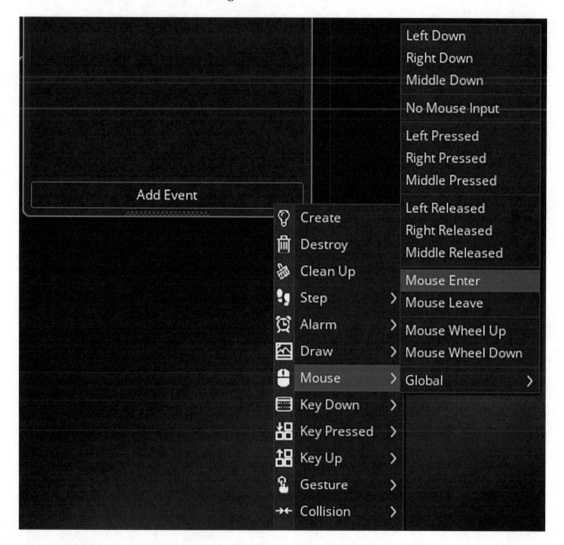

Figure A-52. *Showing location of mouse enter event*

Pop in the following code, which will play the given each time the mouse cursor enters the button area:

```
/// @description play a sound
audio_play_sound(snd_menu_hover,1,false);
```

Next we'll do something similar, create a **Mouse Leave Event**, which is below the **Mouse Enter Event** shown back in Figure A-52.

The code for this Event is

```
/// @description play a sound
audio_play_sound(snd_menu_leave,1,false);
```

The final event is a Mouse Left Pressed Event, which can be located, as shown in Figure A-53.

Figure A-53. *Showing mouse left pressed event*

We'll also add some code that will play a sound when the mouse clicks over the object. Pop in the following into this **Mouse Left Pressed Event**:

```
/// @description play a sound
audio_play_sound(snd_menu_click,1,false);
```

That's all for this object. Now you need to assign this as a **Parent** of the menu buttons.

281

> **Note**   Parents are a great way to allow code and events to happen in a lot of objects. You can assign a parent to an object, and apply something to all its children. It saves on having the code in multiple places. It makes the game design easier, tidier and allows for quick updating or changing of code.

Open up **obj_menu_play**, and click **Parent** then select the object **obj_menu_parent** that you just created, as shown in the Figure A-54.

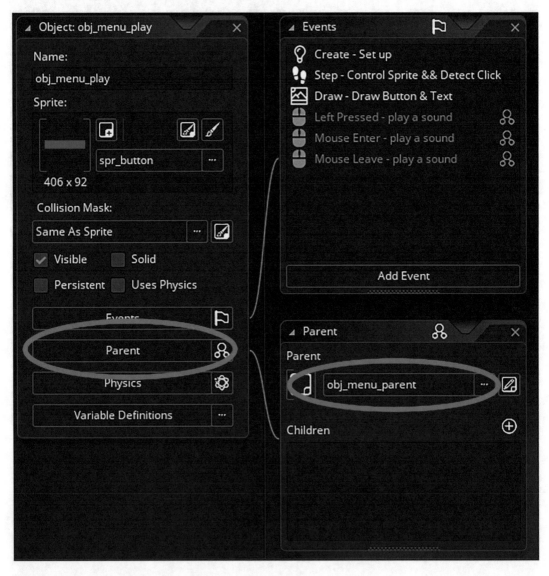

Figure A-54. *Showing how to assign a parent*

Repeat the exact same process for object **obj_menu_info** and **obj_menu_quit**.

That's all the parents set. If you now reopen **obj_menu_parent**, so you'll be able to see it's children objects that it is the parent of, as shown in Figure A-55.

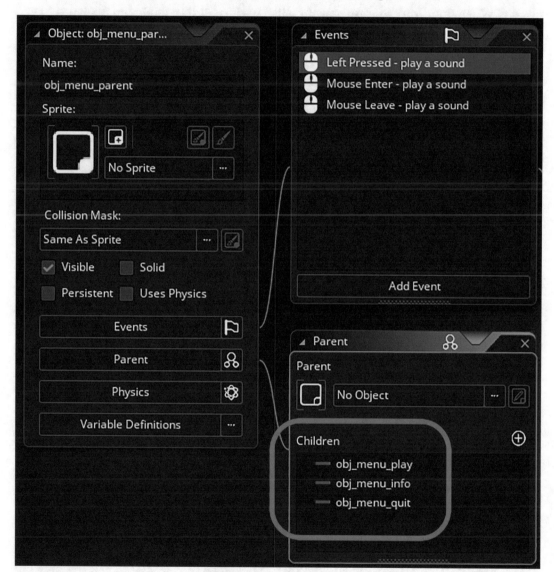

Figure A-55. *Showing the children assigned to obj_menu_parent*

Now is a great point to save and test. You'll now have a functioning menu, and some basic effects.

Next we'll set up enemy planes to have a parent object. Create a new object **obj_enemy_parent**. Then open each of the three enemy objects, **obj_enemy_1**, **obj_enemy_2**, and **obj_enemy_3** have this as their parent. This is the same process as you just did. When done, **obj_enemy_parent** will have its children as shown in Figure A-56.

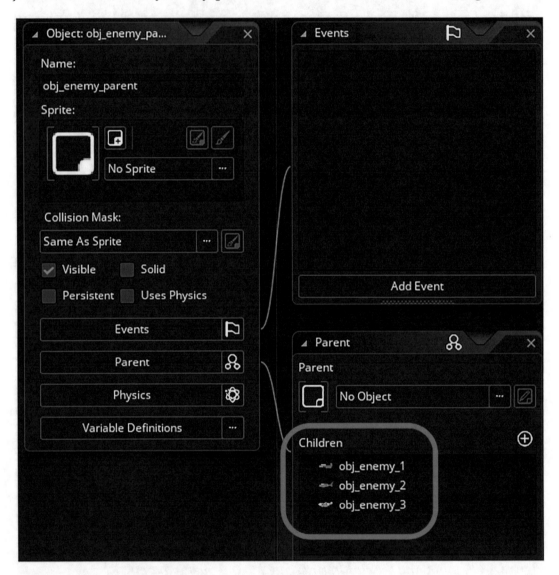

Figure A-56. *Showing parent object with children*

Next we'll repeat this process by creating a parent object for the player's bullet objects.

Create a new object **obj_player_bullet_parent**. Open up **obj_player_bullet** and set the parent object, then do the same with **obj_player_special**.

When done, **obj_player_bullet_parent** will look like that shown in Figure A-57.

Figure A-57. *Showing obj_player_bullet_parent with children assigned*

Next we'll set up the enemy being shot by the player. Open up the parent object, **obj_enemy_parent** and make a **Collision Event with obj_player_bullet_parent**, as shown in Figure A-58. This event will be triggered when any enemy is hit by any player projectile – all nice and tidy in one place, thanks to the power of parents.

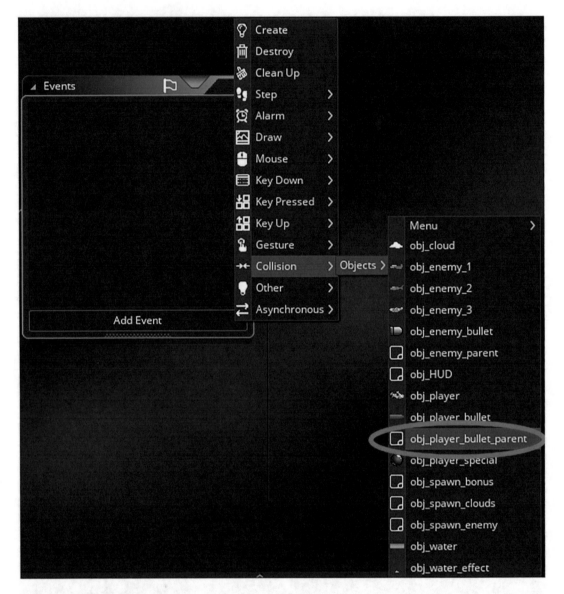

Figure A-58. *Showing setting up of collision event*

Pop in the following code. This will increase the player's hit tally, destroy the colliding projectile instance, create an effect, play a sound, increase the score, and reduce the hp. It will then check the hp value to see if the plane is dead, if it is dead, more points are added, a sound is played, and a few effects created, then destroy the instance.

```
/// @description Hit control
global.hits++;//increase hit count
effect_create_above(ef_explosion,x,y,5,c_red);
audio_play_sound(snd_enemy_hit,1,false);
score++;//increase the player's score
with (other) instance_destroy();//destroy colliding bullet
hp--;//reduce the enemies hp
//check hp and react accordingly
if hp<=0
{
        global.kills++;//increase kill count
        score+=10;//add some more points;
        audio_play_sound(snd_enemy_is_dead,1,false);//play an
                                                additional sound
        //create some more effects
        effect_create_above(ef_smoke,x-20,y+20,5,c_yellow);
        effect_create_above(ef_smoke,x-20,y-20,5,c_yellow);
        effect_create_above(ef_smoke,x+20,y+20,5,c_yellow);
        effect_create_above(ef_smoke,x+20,y-20,5,c_yellow);
        instance_destroy();//destroy self
}
```

That's all for this object.

Next open up **obj_player** and make a **Collision Event with obj_enemy_bullet**, and pop in this code:

```
/// @description Hit by enemy bullet
with (other) instance_destroy();//destroy colliding bullet
health-=5;//reduce player's health
audio_play_sound(snd_player_hit,1,false);
effect_create_above(ef_smokeup,x,y,5,c_red);//create an effect
```

When done, this will look like Figure A-59.

287

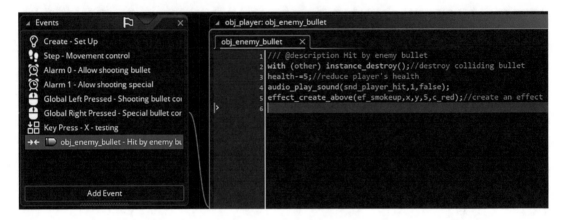

Figure A-59. Showing collision with obj_enemy_bullet with code added

Next open up **obj_enemy_bullet** and add a **Collision Event with obj_player_bullet_parent** with the following code:

```
/// @description hit control
audio_play_sound(snd_metal,1,false);
//calculate mid point between this and colliding instance
var pos_x=(x+other.x)/2;
var pos_y=(y+other.y)/2;
effect_create_above(ef_ring,pos_x,pos_y,5,c_gray);//do effect
//destroy self & colliding instance
with (other) instance_destroy();
instance_destroy();
```

When added in, it will look like that shown in Figure A-60.

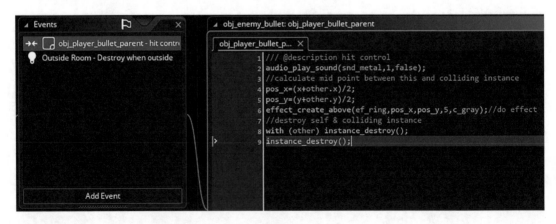

Figure A-60. Showing collision event for bullets

That's all for this object.

Next we'll make an effect for when a player's projectile hits the water.

Open **obj_water** and make a **Collision Event with obj_player_bullet_parent**, with the following code:

```
/// @description water
instance_create_layer(other.x,700,"water",obj_water_effect);
with (other) instance_destroy();//destroy the bullet
```

which when added will look like that shown in Figure A-61.

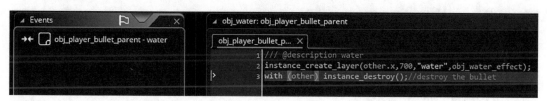

Figure A-61. *Showing code to make a water effect*

That's all for this object.

Open up object **obj_enemy_1** and change the **Alarm 0 Event** code to the following, then add an additional line of code to play a sound when an enemy bullet is created.

```
/// @description Create bullet and restart alarm
alarm[0]=game_get_speed(gamespeed_fps)*3;
//create bullet and set direction, image angle and speed
bullet=instance_create_layer(x,y,"bullets",obj_enemy_bullet);
bullet.direction=180;
bullet.image_angle=180;
bullet.speed=3;
audio_play_sound(snd_enemy_bullet,1,false);
```

Also open up **obj_enemy_2** and change the **Alarm 0 Event**, again adding an extra line to play a sound:

```
/// @description Create bullet and restart alarm
alarm[0]=game_get_speed(gamespeed_fps)*3;
//create bullet and set direction, image angle and speed
var bullet=instance_create_layer(x,y,"bullets",obj_enemy_bullet);
var dir=point_direction(x,y,obj_player.x,obj_player.y);
bullet.direction=dir;
```

```
bullet.image_angle=dir;
bullet.speed=3;
audio_play_sound(snd_enemy_bullet,1,false);
```

Finally open up object **obj_enemy_3**'s **Alarm 0 Event**, and change it to that shown as follows, which will play a different sound when enemy creates it's volley of bullets:

```
/// @description Create bullet and restart alarm
alarm[0]=game_get_speed(gamespeed_fps)*5;
//create bullet and set direction, image angle and speed
var start_angle=-20;
repeat(5)
{
    var bullet=instance_create_layer(x,y,"bullets",obj_enemy_bullet);
    //spawn the bullet
    bullet.speed=4;//set the speed of bullet
    bullet.direction=image_angle-start_angle+180;//match direction to
                                                   that of the plane
    bullet.image_angle=image_angle-start_angle+180;//make the bullet
                                                     point to direction of
                                                     movement
    start_angle+=10;
}
audio_play_sound(snd_enemy_bullet_big,1,false);
```

The final object to update for audio is **obj_player.** Open the **Global Left Mouse Button Pressed Event** and change it so it also plays the bullet sound when it fires a bullet:

```
/// @description Shooting bullet control
if can_shoot_bullet
{
    bullet=instance_create_layer(x,y,"bullets",obj_player_bullet);
    //spawn the bullet
    bullet.speed=4;//set the speed of bullet
    bullet.direction=image_angle;//match direction to that of the plane
    bullet.image_angle=image_angle;//make the bullet point to direction
                                    of movement
    can_shoot_bullet=false;
```

```
alarm[0]= game_get_speed(gamespeed_fps);
global.shots_fired++;//update shot count
audio_play_sound(snd_player_bullet,1,false);
}
```

And then open up the **Global Right Mouse Button Pressed Event** and set the code so that it first checks whether the player can shoot and, if no ammo available, it plays a small no ammo sound. It will then spawn the bullets and play the ammo sound if the player has bullets available to shoot.

```
/// @description Special bullet control
if can_shoot_special && global.special_weapon<00
{
    audio_play_sound(snd_no_ammo,1,false);
}
if can_shoot_special && global.special_weapon>0
{
    audio_play_sound(snd_player_special,1,false);
    global.special_weapon--;//reduce available weapons
    var start_angle=-30;
    can_shoot_special=false;//set flag so cant shoot again
    alarm[1]= game_get_speed(gamespeed_fps);//set alarm to allow
                                        shooting again
    repeat(7)
    {
        var bullet=instance_create_layer(x,y,"bullets",obj_player_
        special);//spawn the bullet
        bullet.speed=4;//set the speed of bullet
        bullet.direction=image_angle-start_angle;//match direction to
                                        that of the plane
        bullet.image_angle=image_angle-start_angle;//make the bullet
                                        point to direction
                                        of movement
        start_angle+=10;
        global.shots_fired++;//update shot count
    }
}
```

Finally open up **obj_bonus** and its **Collision Event** code to

```
/// @description Reset special weapon
global.special_weapon=5;
audio_play_sound(snd_bonus_pick_up,1,false);
instance_destroy();
```

Now is an ideal point to save and test the game so far. You now have a functioning weapon system and some audio effects when shooting.

So go ahead and play the game name and check that everything is working as planned and expected.

Check if

- Menu buttons all work and interact with the mouse as they should.

- Player can fire projectiles (if available).

- Enemy's flying in the pattern they should.

- Enemy's bullet spawn and point in the right direction.

- Sound effects are played when they should.

- Effects spawn in the correct position.

- Enemies can lose hp when hit by player's projectiles.

- Player can lose health, lives, and go to gameover room when out of lives.

- Gameover room shows player stats.

- Game difficulty is set at right level to make it fun, yet challenging.

You should find that everything is correct and working as expected, except the final item. You'll find that it spawns the enemies far too quickly, so let's correct that now.

Open up object **obj_spawn_enemy** and change its **Alarm 0 Event** so it spawns a plane every 14 seconds, as shown in the following:

```
/// @description Call script and reset alarm
spawn_enemy();
alarm[0]= game_get_speed(gamespeed_fps)*14;
```

If you save and test again, you'll find it's more manageable to play.

Congratulations – You've Just Made Your First Game!

APPENDIX B

Programming Challenges

Now you've worked through all the chapters, completed all the assignments, and created your first game, let's take you to the next level.

What now follows are 65 programming challenges to take the Plane Game project to the next level.

I won't be holding your hand this time around, you'll be provided an outline of what you need to achieve, and a screenshot showing it in action.

I'll provide additional functions that you may need to complete each challenge, it's up to you to look in the manual to learn how the function works.

Note You can click the middle-mouse-button when hovering over the GML function in the IDE to open the manual page for that function.

There are also some notes that will point you in the right direction for solving the challenge. In the top left, I've noted the difficulty of the challenge, either **Easy**, **Medium**, or **Hard**.

I've set this up in a way that you can tackle any of these challenges in any order you wish, so, for example, you can do **Challenge 45** then **Challenge 21**.

Each challenge starts with the **Plane Game** project which you just worked through. Just import this and start your choice of Challenge.

If you really get stuck, there is a project file showing an example solution, for example, **Challenge 10.YYZ**.

Note For each challenge, the GML code that applies to the example solution has been commented with ///Challenge code. You can easily search for this using **Edit>>Search & Replace** or **CTRL+SHIFT+F**, and popping **///Challenge code** into the box.

© Ben Tyers 2023
B. Tyers, *GameMaker Fundamentals*, https://doi.org/10.1007/978-1-4842-8713-2

Good luck, and I hope you enjoy your newfound programming skills, and in the future make some awesome games.

CHALLENGE 1 – Slowly Increase Score

EASY

Project Outline: Rather than adding all points at once when an enemy plane is killed, add the points to the score every half second. Also change the score color to red while this happens, and play a coin sound each time a point is added.

Useful Functions: No new functions needed to approach this challenge.

Notes to Help: Make a new a custom score variable target_score and compare and increment this value relative to score value. Combine this with an alarm and you should be good to go.

Screenshot:

CHALLENGE 2 – Mouse over Menu Buttons

EASY

**Project
Outline:**
Change the menu buttons so that Corrected.

When the mouse is over a button, the button and text size increase. Rather than editing each button's Draw Event, create a parent object for all the buttons and set the drawing in this object.

**Useful
Functions:**
image_xscale
image_yscale

Notes to Help: Change the x and y scale to increase the button size, for the text size increase use a different font.

Screenshot:

CHALLENGE 3 – Planes on Menu

MEDIUM

Project Outline:	Make the menu screen more visually appealing by randomly flying planes of different colors from each side of the room. Do this using an alarm. Make some go above the menu buttons and some below. Be sure to destroy them once they have left the room. Use one object for all planes.
Useful Functions:	**choose( )**

choose

Notes to Help:	Choose a different sprite each time you spawn an instance. Create an extra layer below and above the menu button's layer for spawning the instance. Create a new control object to handle the spawning.

Screenshot:

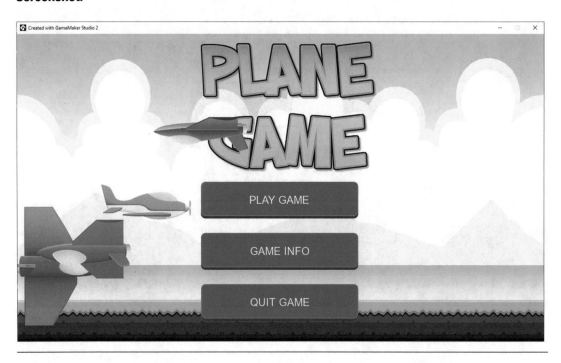

CHALLENGE 4 – Weapon Trail Effects

MEDIUM

Project Outline: Create a smoke trail effect for each of the game's projectiles, with a different sprite for each. Set this to reduce in size and fade.

Useful Functions: draw_sprite_ext

Notes to Help: One approach is to use a single object for all effect trials and set the sprite when spawning it. Create instances of these in succession using an alarm. Use a step event on the effect object to reduce the size and alpha – remember to destroy when faded.

Screenshot:

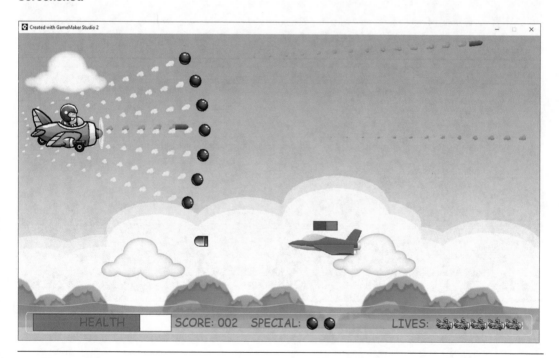

CHALLENGE 5 – Random Game Play

EASY

**Project
Outline:**
The game is currently set up so the plane spawning sequence of the enemies is the same each time. Set it up so the player gets a difference sequence each time they play.

**Useful
Functions:**
randomize( );

Notes to Help: An appropriate random function at game start is all you need for this.

Screenshot:

CHALLENGE 6 – Bonus Bird

EASY

Project Outline: Make a bonus bird fly around the room every once in a while.
If the player shoots it, award 100 bonus points.

Useful Functions: path_start( );

Notes to Help: Use an alarm for spawning, and a path to make it fly around the room a bit
and then leave and destroy itself.

Screenshot:

CHALLENGE 7 – Voice on New Highscore

EASY

Project Outline: On the gameover screen, play a voice message if the player gets a new highscore.

Useful Functions: audio_play_sound( );

Notes to Help: I've included a sound resource for you to use in the resources folder.

Screenshot:

CHALLENGE 8 – Weather Effects

EASY

Project Outline: Periodically make it rain or snow. Set up a timeline to manage this.

Useful Functions: ef_create_above( );

Notes to Help: Standard effects are all that is needed for this challenge.

Screenshot:

CHALLENGE 9 – Player Auto Move

EASY

Project Outline: When key W or S is not pressed, move the player to middle Y position

Useful Functions: No new functions needed to approach this challenge.

Notes to Help: Move up or down based on difference from the midpoint variable.

Screenshot:

CHALLENGE 10 – Music Control

EASY

Project Outline: Add some additional music tracks, use a different one for game and game info rooms. Make a function that stops any music that is currently playing, and start a given music track on loop.

Useful Functions: audio_play_sound( );
audio_stop_sound( );

Notes to Help: Set the function to take in a sound asset and use that to play the sound.

Screenshot:

CHALLENGE 11 – End of Level Boss

MEDIUM

Project Outline: After each sortie of 18 planes, and when they have been destroyed, create an end of level boss. Make this a big boss that moves and fires in a preset pattern. Use a timeline to fire projectiles, and a path for boss movement.

Useful Functions: instance_exists( );

Notes to Help: To keep things tidy, consider using a path for the boss's movement, and a timeline for the spawning of its projectiles.

Screenshot:

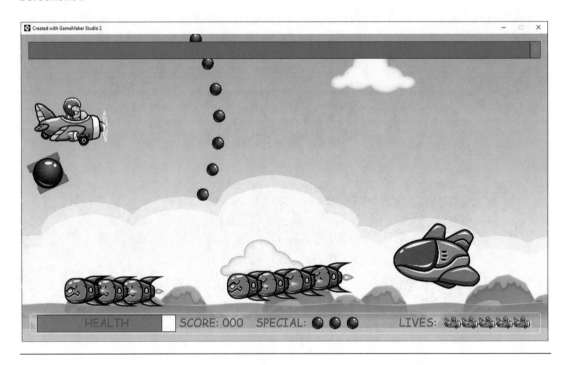

CHALLENGE 12 – Bonus Round

MEDIUM

Project Outline: After the sortie of planes, and when they have all been destroyed, take the player to a bonus round. Set up to spawn and move balloons around the room. The player should have one minute to shoot as many balloons as possible. Set an animation when it is destroyed.

Useful Functions: instance_count( );

Notes to Help: Keep a check using a flag for when sortie has finished – also remember to check if any enemies are present before going to the bonus room.

Screenshot:

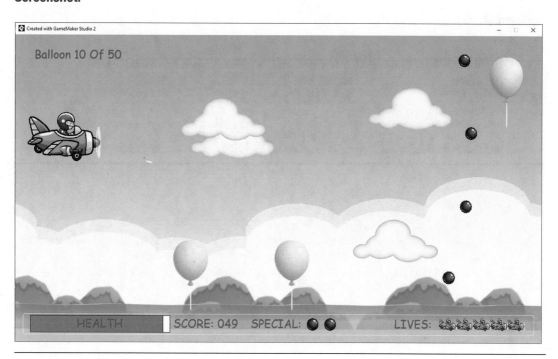

CHALLENGE 13 – Draw Score As Text

VERY HARD

Project Outline:	On the gameover screen, draw the player's score as words instead of numbers. Set this up as a function that takes in a value and returns a string.
Useful Functions:	array[ ]; mod div
Notes to Help:	You'll need to think logically for this. Break down the numbers from the score as you would say them out loud – use this as a base for constructing the required text. You'll only need basic math operators such as MOD and DIV. Use an array to set up the words relative to the location in the array.

Screenshot:

Your Score eight thousand five hundred and two
New HighScore
Shots Fired 35
Shots Hit 2
Kills 0

CHALLENGE 14 – New Enemy

MEDIUM

Project Outline: Create a new enemy that comes in the room, does a full barrel-roll and then exits the screen. Set it to shoot as it flies. Only have this appear twice in any sortie of 18 planes (20 including these extra two added). Use one of the animated planes from the YoYo Games resources folder.

Useful Functions: No new functions needed to approach this challenge.

Notes to Help: Use a combination of a path and sprite control to complete this task. Ensure the bullets it fires start at the front of the plane, taking into account its current image_angle.

Screenshot:

CHALLENGE 15 – Sliding Menu Buttons

MEDIUM

Project Outline: Slide in menu buttons using a sequence. Also add a different effect for each button as it slides into its correct position.

Useful Functions: No new functions needed to approach this challenge.

Notes to Help: Try some other options available, like rotation. Use a sequence for this.

Screenshot:

CHALLENGE 16 – Enemy Crash in Water

EASY

Project Outline: Change the enemy planes so that when they have no HP left they drop into the water and create a splash effect and play a sound. Use a different sound and animation than the ones in the current plane project.

Useful Functions: No new functions needed to approach this challenge.

Notes to Help: Use a variable to determine if the enemy is alive or dead, and act accordingly. Make a new object for the falling sprite, and send through the current plane sprite when you create it.

Screenshot:

CHALLENGE 17 – Shield Bonus

EASY

Project Outline: Make a shield bonus that, when collected, the player cannot take damage for 30 seconds. Show an appropriate visual effect to show it's active.

Useful Functions: No new functions needed to approach this challenge.

Notes to Help: A simple flag and alarm system is needed, check the state of the flag on collision to determine whether the player takes damage or not.

Screenshot:

CHALLENGE 18 – Room Fade In/Out Effect

EASY

Project Outline: Make a fade out and fade in effect when transitioning between rooms. Make it so the room goes black before going to the next room, then fade from black in that room.

Useful Functions: draw_sprite_ext

Notes to Help: You can draw a simple rectangle in black and set its alpha value. Use an alarm system to make a small pause before going to the new room – to allow the fading to fully transition.
Use a different object for fading in and out.

Screenshot:

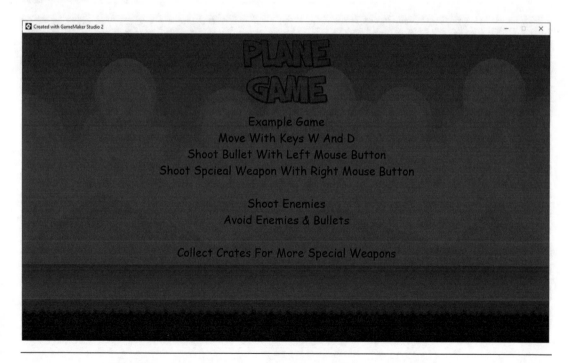

CHALLENGE 19 – Laser Weapon

MEDIUM

Project Outline: Create a laser weapon that the player can fire using the middle mouse button. Limit how often this can be used. Make a small HUD detail in the top left to show its availability. Make a graphical effect if the laser hits an enemy. Allow lasers to pass through all enemies while causing damage.

Useful Functions: No new functions needed to approach this challenge.

Notes to Help: A simple spawning system, a variable with an alarm and a collision event is all you should need for this challenge.

Screenshot:

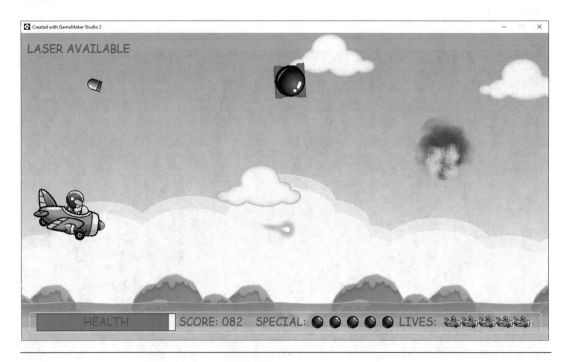

CHALLENGE 20 – Radar Showing Enemies

MEDIUM

Project Outline: Draw on an on screen radar that shows the enemy's position, relative to the player.

Useful Functions: lengthdir_x( );
lengthdir_y( );

Notes to Help: Calculate distance and angle from player to enemy, use these values (dividing the distance as needed) with lengthdir_x( ); and lengthdir_y( ); to draw blips in the right place. Use some basic drawing functions to draw the radar background.

Screenshot:

CHALLENGE 21 – Floating Score Text

EASY

Project Outline: Set up so when an enemy dies floating text appears showing the score earned.

Useful Functions:
draw_text_ext_transformed( );
sin

Notes to Help: Make a new object to handle the drawing of this effect.

Screenshot:

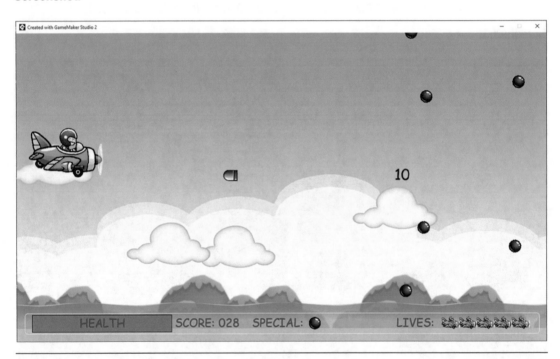

CHALLENGE 22 – Knockback When Shooting

MEDIUM

Project Outline: Make a knock-back effect to the player's plane when it fires its special weapon.

Useful Functions: No new functions needed to approach this challenge.

Notes to Help: A timeline telling the plane how to move would be perfect for this challenge.

Screenshot:

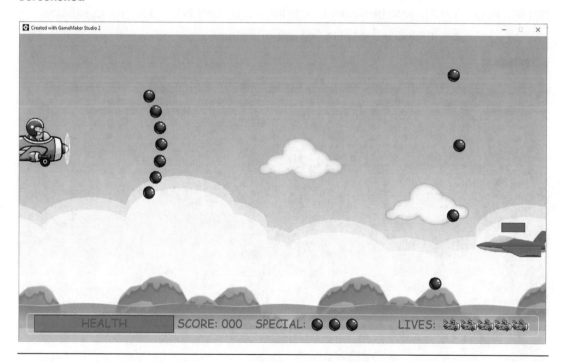

CHALLENGE 23 – Player Flash When Hit

EASY

Project Outline: Make the player or enemy plane briefly flash red when hit by a projectile. Create a new parent object for the enemies and the player, use this to control this effect.

Useful Functions: draw_sprite_ext( )

Notes to Help: You'll need to temporally change the image_blend or use draw_sprite_ext. Use this in combination with a flag and an alarm.

Screenshot:

CHALLENGE 24 – Read Score As Voice

VERY HARD

Project Outline: Convert the integer score to spoken audio, reading the score as you would speak it, when the player reaches the gameover screen.

Useful Functions: array[]

ds_list

Notes to Help: You'll need to queue the sound files and play them in order, a ds_list is suitable for this.

If you have completed challenge 13, you can use this as a starting point.

Screenshot:

CHALLENGE 25 – Mouse Cursor Change

EASY

Project Outline:	Make the mouse cursor change its type when over or not over a menu button.
Useful Functions:	window_set_cursor( );
Notes to Help:	You can add this control to current mouse enter and leave events.
Screenshot:	

CHALLENGE 26 – Shooting Cool Down

MEDIUM

Project Outline: Create a firing cool down system for the player's main bullet. Set it so if the player shoots too quickly, they will have to wait for it to be replenished before they can shoot again. Draw some text over a bar to show its current state.

Useful Functions: No new functions needed to approach this challenge.

Notes to Help: Use a couple of flags and alarms as a control for this. You can draw a couple of rectangles to show current availability of the primary weapon.

Screenshot:

CHALLENGE 27 – Basic Weapon Upgrade

MEDIUM

Project Outline: Make weapon bonus upgrade the player can collect. Make it so the player's primary weapon fires two shots, limit how long this upgrade lasts for.

Useful Functions: No new functions needed to approach this challenge.

Notes to Help: A simple alarm system and flag is all you need to keep track of the upgrade.

Screenshot:

CHALLENGE 28 – Mega Weapon

EASY

Project Outline: Make a bonus collectable that destroys all enemies on screen.

Useful Functions: with( );

Notes to Help: You can use the with function to apply code to the parent of all enemies.

Screenshot:

CHALLENGE 29 – Hoop to Fly Through

HARD

Project Outline: Make a hoop that the player can fly through, award 50 points each time they do.

Useful Functions: No new functions needed to approach this challenge.

Notes to Help: In the resources there is a hoop sprite consisting of a front and back image. You'll need each half on a different layer, one behind the player and one in front, so the player can fly through it. Change the collision mask to detect when the player flies through it.

Screenshot:

CHALLENGE 30 – Coins Bonuses

EASY

Project Outline: Spawn a pattern of coins that the player can collect and increase their score. Use a timeline for this.

Useful Functions: No new functions needed to approach this challenge.

Notes to Help: Call the timeline periodically to spawn a preset sequence of coins.

Screenshot:

CHALLENGE 31 – Logo Change Color

EASY

Project Outline: Make the menu logo color change between blue and red color.

Useful Functions: draw_sprite_ext( );

Notes to Help: Use two premade sprites, and fade between them to make this effect.

Screenshot:

CHALLENGE 32 – Friendly Hot Air Balloon

EASY

Project Outline: Make a hot air balloon spawn every now and then. Set the player to lose health if they hit it with a projectile. Make it flash red when hit.

Useful Functions: No new functions needed to approach this challenge.

Notes to Help: A simple spawn system and some path variants would be good here. Change the collision mask to only cover the main part of the balloon.

Screenshot:

CHALLENGE 33 – Water-Based Enemy

EASY

Project Outline: Make an additional water-based enemy that moves across the bottom of the screen. Make it shoot at the player.

Useful Functions: No new functions needed to approach this challenge.

Notes to Help: Update the existing spawn system and create a new object.

Screenshot:

CHALLENGE 34 – Dangerous Blimp

EASY

Project Outline: Make a blimp that occasionally flies across the screen. Set the player to lose health if they collide with it. Make it move up and down a bit as it crosses the room.

Useful Functions: No new functions needed to approach this challenge.

Notes to Help: Create some visual system so the player knows they are taking damage.

Screenshot:

CHALLENGE 35 – Difficulty Settings

HARD

Project Outline:	After the player clicks play game, take to a new room that allows to select a difficulty from Easy, Medium, and Hardest. Also set up that there are three highscores available, one for each difficultly. Draw all three best scores on the gameover screen. Adjust some game alarms to reflect the difficulty.
Useful Functions:	No new functions needed to approach this challenge.
Notes to Help:	You can duplicate a current button, and edit for a new purpose. Change the alarms to get shorter, based on difficulty setting.
Screenshot:	

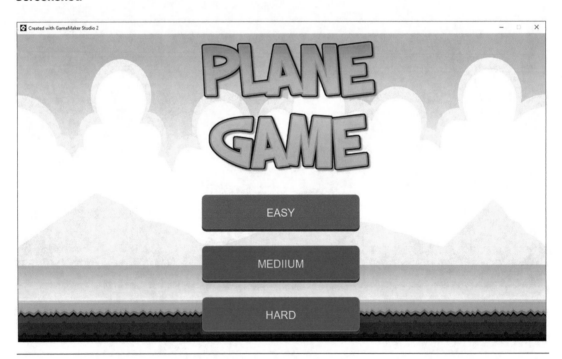

CHALLENGE 36 – Fast Move Bonus

EASY

Project Outline: Make a bonus that temporally allows the player to move up and down at twice its normal speed.

Useful Functions: No new functions needed to approach this challenge.

Notes to Help: A simple flag and alarm are all you need for this. Tweak the player movement code to reflect if this upgrade is current.

Screenshot:

CHALLENGE 37 – Exploding Mega Bomb

EASY

Project Outline:	Make a new bomb weapon. Do it so it moves to the middle of the room and explodes, creating a circle of moving mini mines that can damage the enemies. Allow middle-mouse button to spawn it.

Useful Functions:	move_towards_point( );
	 distance_to_point( );
	 for( );

Notes to Help:	Make it move to the center (remember that depending on its speed to the center of the room it may be a few pixels off – account for this.) and use a suitable loop to spawn 36 mini mines separated by 10' angle.

Screenshot:

CHALLENGE 38 – Combo Kill Effect

EASY

Project Outline: Make a system that shows a double or triple for the player killing enemies in quick succession. Show visually when player does this.

Useful Functions: No new functions needed to approach this challenge.

Notes to Help: An alarm system and some flags would suit well here. Assets are in the Message asset folder

Screenshot:

CHALLENGE 39 – Slowly Change Menu Button Size

EASY

**Project
Outline:** Make the menu button slowly increase in size when the mouse is over, and slowly reduce back to starting size when leaving. Move all drawing code to the button parent.

**Useful
Functions:** event_inherited( );
draw_sprite_ext( );
draw_text_tranformed( );
clamp( );

Notes to Help: Have one variable for both button and text sizes. Apply the changes to the button parent object.

Screenshot:

CHALLENGE 40 – Double Damage

EASY

Project Outline: Make the player's special cause twice its current damage to enemies.

Useful Functions: No new functions needed to approach this challenge.

Notes to Help: Create a flag according to whether double damage is current. Use an alarm to turn it off.

Screenshot:

CHALLENGE 41 – Wobbly Logo

EASY

Project Outline: Make the logo on the menu screen wobble.

Useful Functions: sin
draw_sprite_ext( )

Notes to Help: Use the sin function to control the angle and size of the image.

Screenshot:

CHALLENGE 42 – Plane Player Crash

MEDIUM

Project Outline: When the player dies, make it crash into the water and make lots of audio and graphical effects, which completes before going to the gameover room.

Useful Functions: No new functions needed to approach this challenge.

Notes to Help: Personally I'd create an extra object for this, changing to it when the player is dead.

Screenshot:

CHALLENGE 43 – Better Collison Detection

EASY

Project Outline: Change the collision masks of the planes so just the main body is a hit area. Also change the projectile's masks to match their sprite shapes.

Useful Functions: No new functions needed to approach this challenge.

Notes to Help: Use the appropriate mask setting best suited to the shape of the planes/ projectiles.

Screenshot:

CHALLENGE 44 – Text with Border

EASY

Project Outline: Draw the HUD text with outlined border. Create a function to handle the drawing.

Useful Functions: draw_get_color( );

Notes to Help: Take in the x and y positions, and the text. Draw the text in black with slightly different positions to draw the border, then draw the text over the top.

Screenshot:

CHALLENGE 45 – How to Play Information

EASY

Project Outline: Scroll some graphics telling the player how to play the game when the main game level starts.

Useful Functions: No new functions needed to approach this challenge.

Notes to Help: Use one object to control the spawning of the info, use another instance to move the information. There are some sprites in the cutscene resources folder that you can use.

Screenshot:

CHALLENGE 46 – Shop System

VERY HARD

Project Outline:
Make a shop where the player can purchase and sell three new weapons. Set up a shop using a mix of text and graphics.

Useful Functions:
No new functions needed to approach this challenge.

Notes to Help:
Use an array to store the weapon data: sprite, object, fire sound, hit sound, and ammo amount and damage. Make some buttons to allow the player to buy and sell these weapons. Make some additional weapons for use in the shop, they don't need to be part of the main game – unless you're up to this additional challenge.

Screenshot:

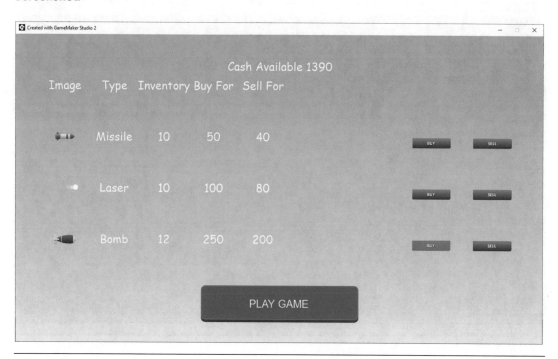

CHALLENGE 47 – On-Screen Keyboard

EASY

Project Outline: Create an on-screen keyboard with buttons the player can click to enter their name. Change the button appearance when the mouse is over a button. Play a sound when a letter is added, or max length is reached. Limit name to 12 characters max.

Useful Functions: No new functions needed to approach this challenge.

Notes to Help: This may look complex, but it is only detecting mouse presses and adjusting a string accordingly. Create a control object to create all the letter buttons.

Screenshot:

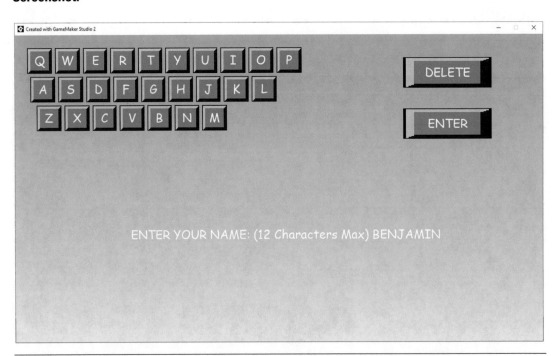

CHALLENGE 48 – Name with Highscore

EASY

Project Outline: Add a name to a highscore. Show this is on the menu screen.

Useful   ini_write_string( );
Functions: ini_read_string( );

Notes to Help: Create a key in your ini file and use that for loading or saving. Use project
                      Challenge 47 as starting point, or use keyboard_get_string( );

Screenshot:

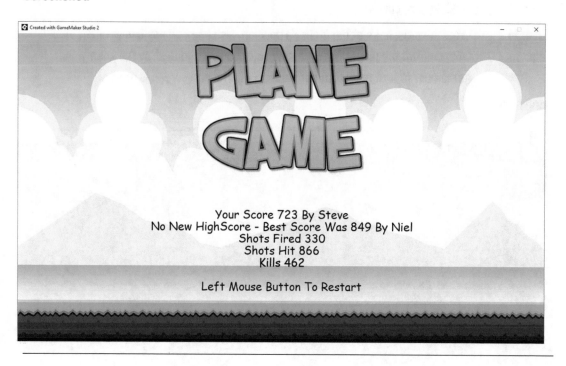

CHALLENGE 49 – Shoot Weapon to Target

EASY

Project Outline: Create a new weapon that fires to the mouse's position. Display a target for this. Allow middle mouse button to fire this. Draw the missile using drawing code instead of a sprite. Make this object kill the enemy with one hit. Hide the mouse cursor in game.

Useful Functions: mouse_x
mouse_y
window_set_cursor( );

Notes to Help: Draw the crosshairs at the mouse's position, also use this position to direct the weapon from the player. Set up a new collision event to destroy the enemy. Remember to turn mouse cursor back on when menu screen is present.

Screenshot:

CHALLENGE 50 – Create Lots of Effects

EASY

Project Outline: When player collects a coin, create a fanfare of sound and graphical effects.

Useful Functions: for ( );

Notes to Help: Use challenge 30 as a starting base if you have already completed it. Use a loop to spawn multiple effects at once.

Screenshot:

CHALLENGE 51 – Increasing Difficulty

EASY

Project Outline: Make the level get progressively harder, by making the planes spawn and shoot gradually faster

Useful Functions: No new functions needed to approach this challenge.

Notes to Help: Use a variable and set it up so when alarms are set they are periodically reduced in length.

Screenshot:

CHALLENGE 52 – Quit Game Confirmation

EASY

Project Outline: When the player selects quit on the menu, ask the player if they are sure – and act accordingly.

Useful Functions: No new functions needed to approach this challenge.

Notes to Help: Duplicate existing buttons, change accordingly and add to a new room.

Screenshot:

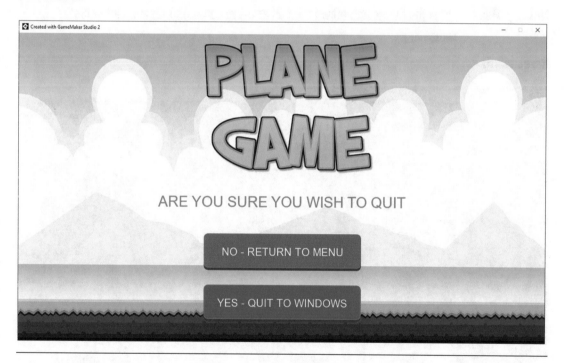

CHALLENGE 53 – Fuel Control System

EASY

Project Outline: Set up a fuel system. Make fuel decrease over time, and faster if keys W or S are pressed. Make a bonus fuel can that restores fuel level to full.
Draw using a gauge. If player runs out of fuel, they lose a life.

Useful Functions: No new functions needed to approach this challenge.

Notes to Help: Draw the gauge and adjust the fuel arrow according to the amount of fuel remaining.

Screenshot:

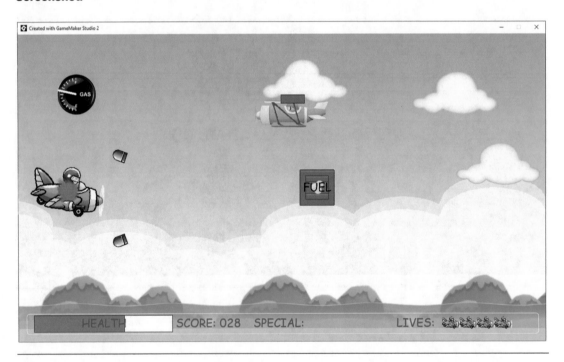

CHALLENGE 54 – Heat Seeking Weapon

EASY

Project Outline: Make a bonus weapon that automatically finds an enemy target.

Useful Functions: instance_exists( );

noone

Notes to Help: Look for target and move toward it, remembering to look for a new target if the current one is destroyed by other means.

Screenshot:

CHALLENGE 55 – Character Selection

EASY

Project Outline: Create a character select room where the player can choose a plane type and color. Set up so this is used for the player in the game level.

Useful Functions: sprite_index;

Notes to Help: You can set and read a sprite with the preceding code. Create four objects, each with a different plane image that can be clicked.

Screenshot:

CHALLENGE 56 – Player Achievements

EASY

Project Outline: Add some achievements, such as 100 kills, 250 points, 1000 shots.
Show this on gameover screen.

Useful Functions: ds_list_add( );
for( )v;

Notes to Help: You can handle all this on the gameover screen. Consider adding strings to a
ds_list so you can draw them on screen.

Screenshot:

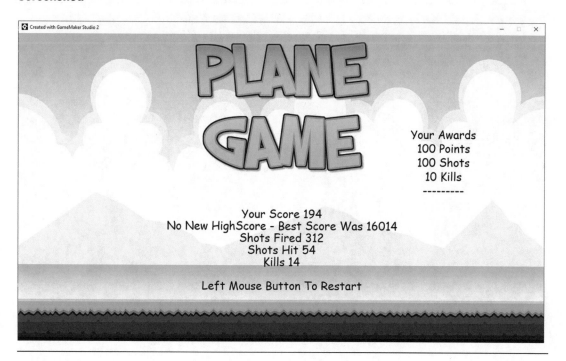

CHALLENGE 57 – Engine Sounds

EASY

Project Outline: Play an engine while the player is moving up or down. Also, set a stutter sound when W or S is released.

Useful Functions: audio_is_playing( )

audio_stop_sound( )

Notes to Help: Some basic audio control is all you need here.

Screenshot:

CHALLENGE 58 – Hit Enemy Damage

EASY

Project Outline: Set it up so the player takes damage if hitting an enemy plane. Show this visually.

Useful Functions: place_meeting( )
draw_sprite_ext( );

Notes to Help: Some simple collision code in the step event would help here. Draw the sprite with an effect if collision is true, use a flag for this.

Screenshot:

CHALLENGE 59 – Mega Super Weapon

EASY

Project Outline: Make a super weapon that the player can shoot once every two minutes. Make this destroy all enemies on screen. Create lots of explosions and effects to show this visually.

Useful Functions: with( )

Notes to Help: Create effects using objects and effect_create_above. Use with() to make damage to all enemy instances. Remember to increase score, according to how many enemies are destroyed – instance_number will help here.

Screenshot:

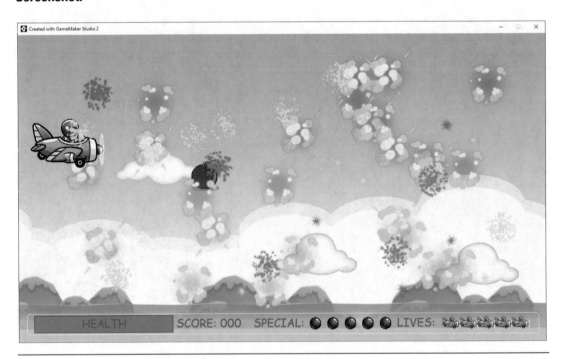

CHALLENGE 60 – Mini Helper Plane

EASY

Project Outline:	Allow player to spawn a mini helper plane that will target and shoot enemy planes. Set it to destroy after 60 seconds. Make it target the y position of an enemy and shoot bullets as it does so.
Useful Functions:	instance_exists noone
Notes to Help:	Spawn on key press, allow it to look to see if an enemy is present, if it is then target it. If a target is destroyed, look for a new target.

Screenshot:

CHALLENGE 61 – Moving Text

EASY

Project Outline: On the game info screen, make the text drop in from the top of the window.

Useful Functions: No new functions needed to approach this challenge.

Notes to Help: Gradually change its y position, stopping at an appropriate location.

Screenshot:

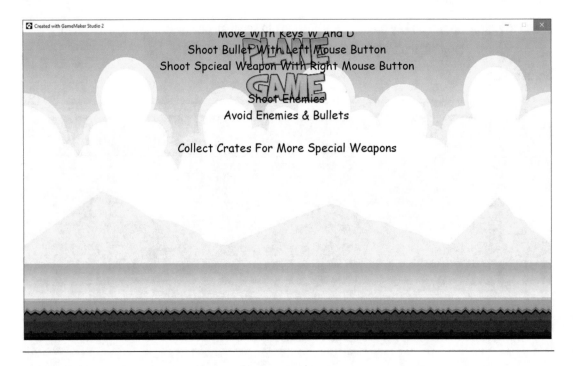

CHALLENGE 62 – Enemy Incoming Alert

EASY

Project Outline: Make an indicator that gives the player advanced warning of incoming planes, for example, a pointing arrow.

Useful Functions: No new functions needed to approach this challenge.

Notes to Help: When spawning an enemy, make note of its y position. Use this to spawn an arrow object on screen, using an alarm to make it show for a brief period of time.

Screenshot:

CHALLENGE 63 – Menu Plane Effect

EASY

Project Outline: On the main menu, set it so a mini plane is on the left of any active button. Make this fade in and out, depending on whether the mouse cursor is over the sprite.

Useful Functions: draw_sprite_ext( );.

Notes to Help: Use a variable that changes based on whether the mouse is over or not. Use this to draw with an alpha value. Make this value change gradually over time.

Screenshot:

CHALLENGE 64 – Heat Distortion Effect

EASY

Project Outline: Set up heat effect for the main game level.

Useful Functions: No new functions needed to approach this challenge.

Notes to Help: Just use the effects layer for this.

Screenshot:

CHALLENGE 65 – Screen Shake

EASY

Project Outline: Make the screen shake for three seconds when the player gets hit by an enemy bullet.

Useful Functions: camera_set_view_pos( );

Notes to Help: You'll need a basic view for this, set the view and port the same size as the room. Use camera functions to temporally change its position.

Screenshot:

APPENDIX C

Purchasing

GameMaker has several subscription tiers available, depending on which platform you plan to publish your final game to.

You can, however, develop your game on the free version and upgrade your subscription when you're ready.

Logging in or Creating a New Account

To start with, you'll need to set up an account at `https://accounts.yoyogames.com/login`

Either login in to an existing account or create a new account (Figure C-1).

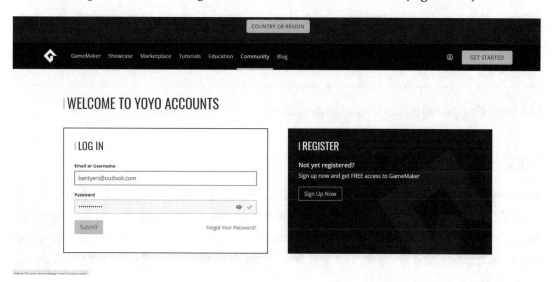

Figure C-1. *Login to existing account or create a new one*

Figure C-2 shows how to set up a new account.

© Ben Tyers 2023
B. Tyers, *GameMaker Fundamentals*, https://doi.org/10.1007/978-1-4842-8713-2

Figure C-2. *Setting up a new account*

Subscription Options

Note   You can always develop and test your game using the Free version, and update your subscription type when you're ready to publish and distribute your game.

The following subscription types are available.

Free

Allows you to use GameMaker and test games, as well as being able to publish on the GXC. GXC is a specialist website browser that allows for playing of games directly through the website. Publishing to this platform is a synch, literally just name your game, add a description and a screenshot and your game is available to play on the GXC. See https://gxc.gg for more information.

Creator

Allows you to use GameMaker and test games, as well as being able to publish on the GXC and desktop exports (Windows, Mac, and Linux).

Indie

Allows you to use GameMaker and test games, as well as being able to publish on the GXC , desktop, web, and mobile exports.

Enterprise

Allows you to use GameMaker and test games, as well as being able to publish on the GXC , desktop, web, and mobile exports.

This option also allows publishing to PlayStation 4, PlayStation 5, Xbox One, Xbox Series X|S, and Nintendo Switch.

Note   To publish to consoles you will require a publisher account with the relevant console publisher.

Summary

For more information on the available options, see https://help.yoyogames.com/hc/en-us/articles/115002637011.

If you are just starting out, I would recommend either the Free option or the Creator option. Figure C-3 shows available options at time of publishing.

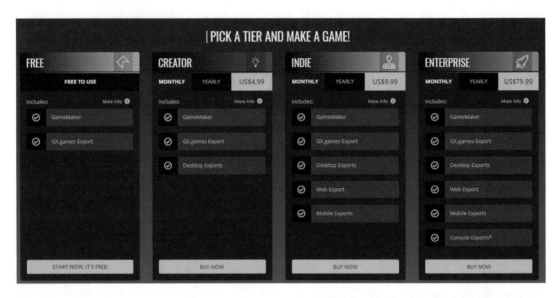

Figure C-3. *Summary of export types*

Once you have subscribed, you'll be able to see your subscription types as shown in Figure C-4.

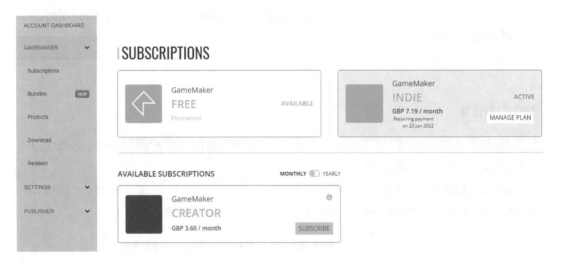

Figure C-4. *Showing your subscriptions*

Installing

Installation is pretty straightforward, just download, double-click, and follow the prompts.

Downloading

Once you have set up your account and chosen your subscription type, the next step is to install GameMaker. Just click the Download tab on the left, as shown in Figure C-5.

Figure C-5. *Showing download options*

Open the download and follow the instructions to install GameMaker.
Once done, open the program.

Staring a New Project

Start a new GML project and name it "Example". As shown in Figure C-6.

Figure C-6. *Starting a new project*

The IDE

The Ide is where you'll develop your game. This appendix and the main chapters will guide you around some of the more commonly used features.

Menus

Figure C-7 shows the main menu.

Figure C-7. *Showing menu*

File

This section allows for file options. You can create a new project, import, export, and set preferences. For now you don't need to do anything, and I suggest not changing any preferences either.

Edit

Allows you to undo or redo an action. You can also search your GML for a given phrase.

Build

This allows you to run your game, or create a package (depending on your subscription type).

Windows

Allows you to set various windows, use of this is not covered in this book.

Tools

Allows for setting various options for your game. You do not need to concern yourself with this section for now.

Marketplace

Allows importing and exporting of marketplace assets.

Layouts

Allows saving or loading a preferred layout of the IDE. You don't need to worry about this option for now.

Help

Various help options.

I suggest opening the manual now and having a look through. The manual is extremely informative, and a great place to look up functions and how to use them. I've been using GameMaker for over ten years and still refer to it from time-to-time.

Source Control

Really for just advanced users/team efforts. This is beyond the scope of this book.

Note   It is strongly recommended that you do not use Google Drive or similar backup/syncing software to save your project file in. This has a strong change of breaking your save file – and once broken, it is near impossible to fix. I do recommend exporting your project file to an additional external drive.

Target

The target option allows you to select the target for your build (Figure C-8). When you create an executable, it will be created for the selected target. Options will differ depending on the subscription package you have.

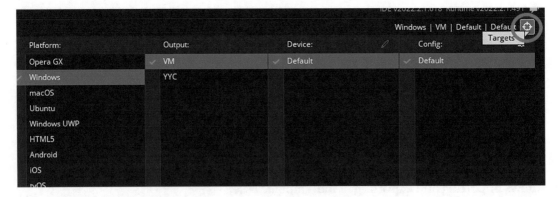

Figure C-8. *Target option*

Assets

On the right-hand side, you'll see the assets. These assets are the elements that make up your game. Most of these are covered within this book, as shown in Figure C-9.

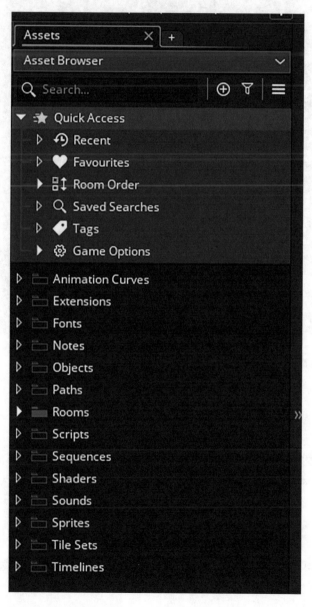

Figure C-9. *Showing the assets*

There are a few ways to create a new asset, one way is to right click the assets area and choose the asset type you would like to create, as shown in Figure C-10.

Figure C-10. *Creating a new asset*

Sprites

Sprites are the graphics that are used in your game. These are used as your objects, backgrounds, and tiles sets.

Importing a Single Image

First create your sprite and give it a name, for example, as shown in Figure C-11.

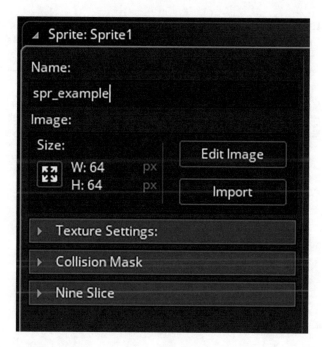

Figure C-11. *Naming a sprite*

If you are just importing a single image, you can just click Import, as shown in Figure C-12.

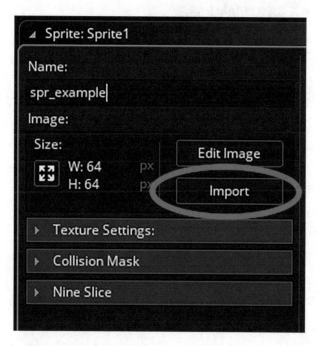

Figure C-12. *Importing a single image*

You can then navigate and select the image you wish to import, for example, as shown in Figure C-13.

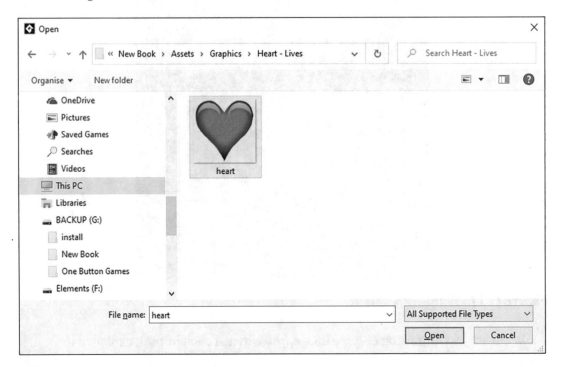

Figure C-13. *Importing a single image*

Importing a Sprite Sheet

To import a sprite sheet, create a new sprite and give it a name, then click edit, as shown in Figure C-14.

Figure C-14. *Editing an image*

Next select Image and then Import Strip Image, as shown in Figure C-15.

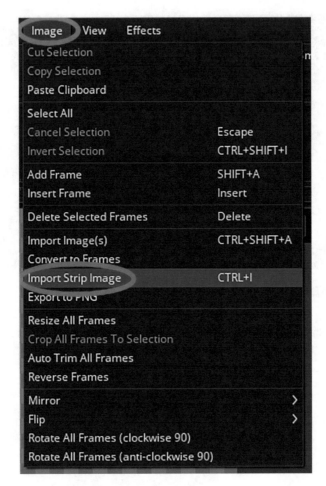

Figure C-15. *Importing a sprite sheet*

Then enter the details for the image as shown in Figure C-16. Typically, this will be the sprites total width divided by the number of images, and similarly for the height.

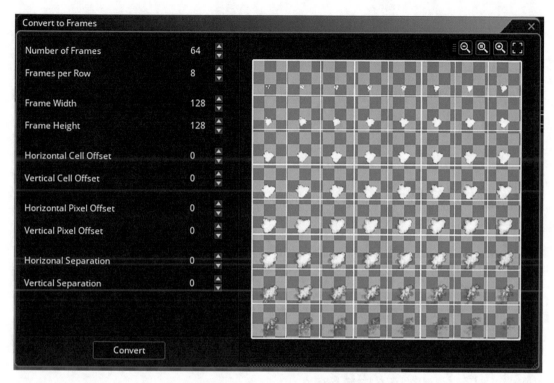

Figure C-16. *Showing import settings for sprite example*

Importing a Sprite Strip

If you have a sprite source that is a strip, for example, as shown in Figure C-17, you can just click the Import button, and it should set up the subimages automatically.

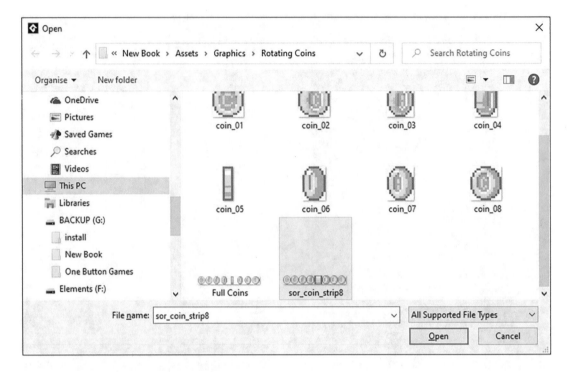

Figure C-17. *Importing a strip image*

Resizing Sprites

Sometimes you'll want to resize the sprites for your game. This can be done with an external editor, prior to importing, or use the sprite editor that's built in to GameMaker.

After importing your sprite, click edit as shown in Figure C-14. Then click Image and then Resize All Frames as shown in Figure C-18.

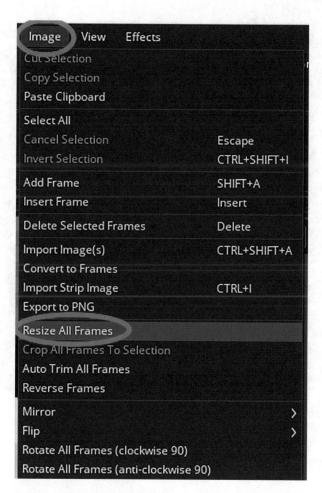

Figure C-18. *Choosing resize all frames*

You can then set your resize options, depending on how you will use the sprite within your game. Figure C-19 shows an example.

Figure C-19. *Showing example resize settings*

Sprite Origin

Sprites also allow you to set the sprite origin. This relates to the location of the sprite where it will be drawn when used within your game. This is dealt with in more detail in Chapter 7 of this book. For now, you can just use the default settings of top-left.

When you do need to change the origin, you can enter the details in the top-right of the sprite info, as shown in Figure C-20.

Figure C-20. *Showing sprite origin options*

Fonts

Sprites are rendered to a texture page upon game compiling; the font does not need to be installed on the game player's computer.

Creating a Font

Figure C-21 shows how to create a font that your game can then use.

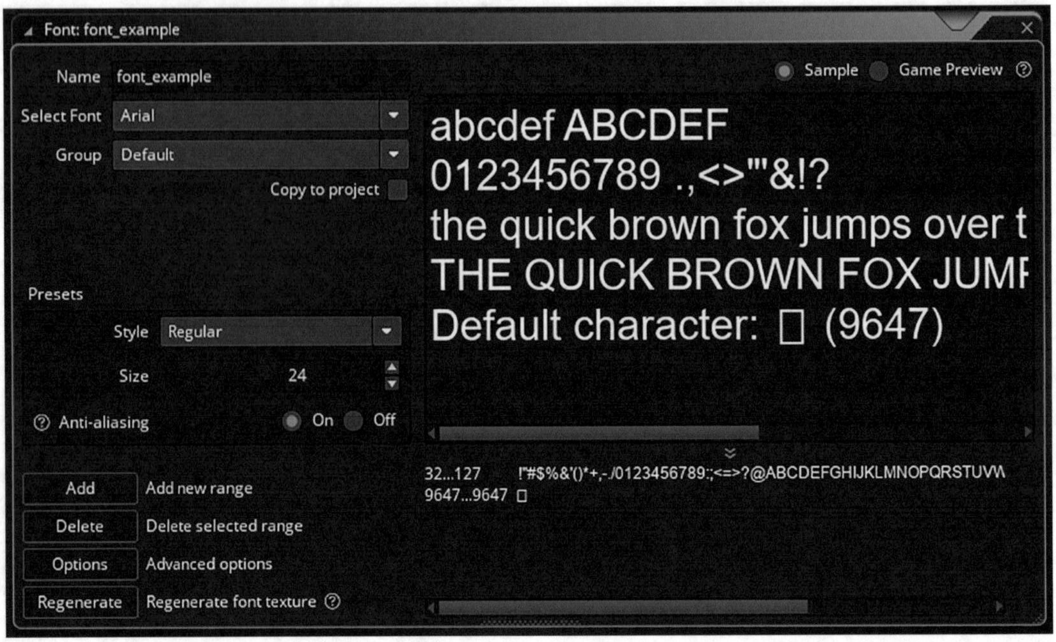

Figure C-21. *Creating a new font*

Note   If you add a new font to your system, you may need to save your game and restart GameMaker before it shows up as an available font.

As with any other asset you're using, game (sprites, audio, etc.), fonts will have licensing terms for use. Some can only be used for non-commercial use, or can be used for commercial use if you make a donation. You should really check the terms for each and every asset used in your game. This is not intended as legal advice,

---

Objects

Objects are the lifeblood of GameMaker. You'll use these to create things like the player's character, enemies, display the HUD, and make and detect interactions between other objects and make things happen; like sound effects, score changes, etc.

Assigning a Sprite

Once you have created your object, you can assign a sprite. Click where shown in Figure C-22.

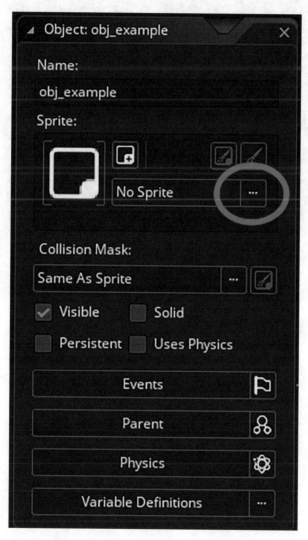

Figure C-22. *Setting a sprite*

You can then navigate to where your sprite is and select it, as shown in Figure C-23.

Figure C-23. *Choosing a loaded sprite*

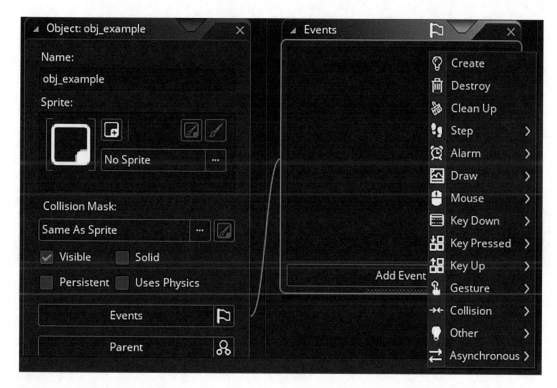

Figure C-24. *Showing events*

Events

Events are things that happen to your objects, you can think of them as triggers that can be used to make your code execute. This book covers the events you're likely to use most often. These are shown in Figure C-24.

Create

This event is run when an instance is created through code or if the instance is already placed in the room, when the room starts. This is a great place to set up the variables needed for your object.

Clean Up

This event is called when the object is no longer required, for example, when changing rooms. You can use this event to remove certain variable types to ensure the memory is cleaned up and made available again. This prevents some memory issues from occurring. This is not covered by this book.

Step

Code in this event is run every step of the game. With default game settings, this happens 60 times per second. This event is typically used for code that you want to continually check, for example, player movement, collisions, and score updating.

Alarm

An alarm is a type of timer. This event will trigger when the alarm has run down to 0. This is great for making code execute at certain times, for example, destroying a bullet two seconds after it has been fired.

Draw

This event is used to draw things like sprites and text. It can also be used to draw geometric shapes, and effects. This book only deals with the main Draw Event.

Note   It is good practice to only place drawing-related code in a Draw Event. Placing non-necessary code may cause your game to slow down.

Mouse

These events deal with mouse interaction.

Note   There is an important difference between the events. Down triggers while the mouse button is being held down, Pressed triggers once when the button is pressed, and Released triggers once when the mouse button is released.

Key Events

These events relate to keyboard input. As with mouse input, there is strong distinction between Down, Pressed, and Released Events.

Note   Mouse and Keyboard Events can also be detected using GML code. This book mainly deals with GML approach.

Gesture

These events are mainly used when creating games for phones and mobile devices which have touch screens.

Collision

This event triggers when two instances collide. You're likely to use this (or it's code alternatives) a lot in your game.

Other

There are some useful events here, some of which are covered in this book. These are shown in Figure C-25.

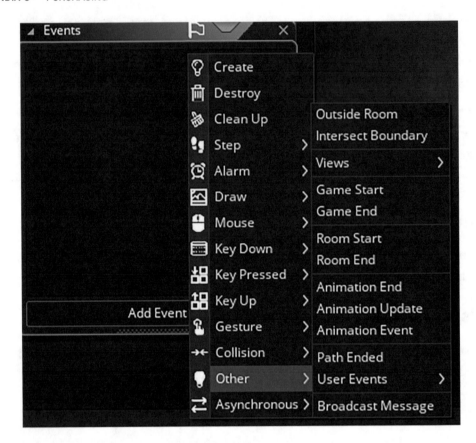

Figure C-25. *Showing other events*

Asynchronous

Asynchronous events are event calls that work as background tasks, and can trigger when the task is complete. Typically used for online actions, such as in app purchases, and loading adverts.

GML Code

Once an event is created, you can enter code, either by typing it in or copy and pasting from another source. Figure C-26 shows some code.

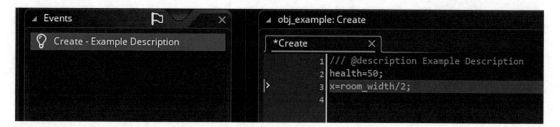

Figure C-26. *Showing some example code*

Sounds

Sounds are the files that will create your game's sound effects and music.

GameMaker supports a number of sound file types:

OGG

WAV

MP3

Depending on how you set up your sound files and the target platform, file types maybe converted to another type when compiling.

Importing

Importing a sound is quite easy. Just create and name a sound, and then click where shown and navigate to where your sound file is located, as shown in Figure C-27.

Figure C-27. *Loading in a sound file*

Sound Settings

You'll also see some sound settings. I suggest using Uncompressed – Not Steamed for short sounds (like sound effects), and Compressed – Not Steamed for music (this will keep the file size of your compiled game much lower). Figure C-28 shows the setting for the example music track.

Figure C-28. *Showing sound settings for a music track*

Rooms

Rooms are where your game's action takes place. This is where you'll add instances of your objects. These could be, for example; your menu, game level, or game information.

Adding Instance

First select an instance layer, for example, as shown in Figure C-29.

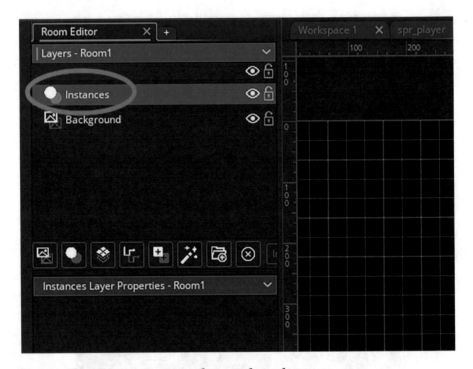

Figure C-29. *Showing an instance layer selected*

Next is drag over and place an instance of an object into the room, see Figure C-30 for this step.

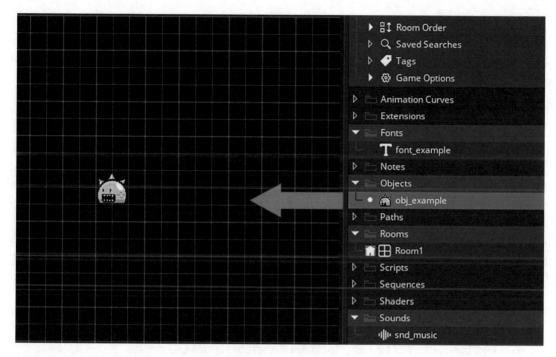

Figure C-30. *Adding an instance to your room*

Note There is an important distinction between objects and instances. When in your resource tree, they are referred to as **objects**. When you place them in your game room, they are referred to as **instances**. Your game may have multiple instances of them in your game room, for example, five enemies in a maze game. Each instance is a separate entity and can be individually referenced to make things happen to it.

Background

You may want to have an image as the background for your room. First create a sprite, for example, bg_room_1, as shown in Figure C-31.

389

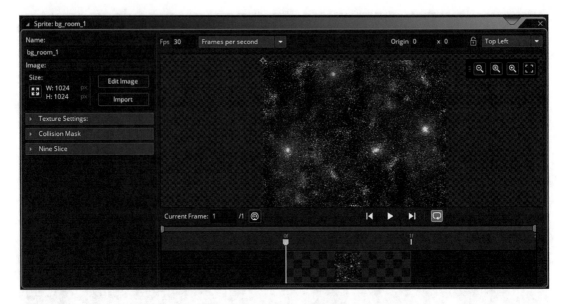

Figure C-31. *Loaded in sprite for background use*

You can then set as the background, as shown in Figure C-32.

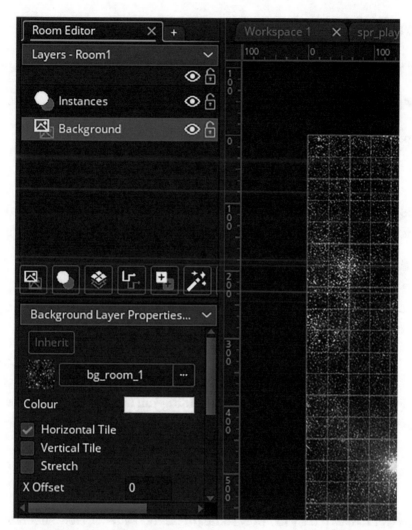

Figure C-32. Setting a background

These will likely be the most used layers in your game.

Layers

You can construct different layers for different uses. Layers are drawn from the bottom to the top. So, in the previous example, the background will be drawn first and the instance of **obj_example** above it.

You can also have multiple layers of the same type, for example, to draw players over other instances, or use multiple backgrounds to create effects such as parallax.

Background

As discussed previously, used for placing background images.

Instances

As shown previously, these are the layers that will hold your object instances.

Tiles

This layer allows placing of tiled sprites, great for designing levels, etc. Using tiles for non-interactive elements will help your game have smaller memory and graphics usage.

Paths

Paths are used for preset movements that your instances can follow. There is a chapter dedicated to this later in the book.

Asset

This layer allows for the placing of images, enabling you to add graphics to the room without having to assign them to an object. Personally, I have never felt the need to use this layer.

Effects

The effects layer makes it easy to apply some predefined effects. New effects are added regularly. These are much easier to use than the Shader counterpart alternative.

Rooms Order

Figure C-33 shows an example with multiple rooms in the asset tree.

Figure C-33. *Showing rooms example*

Note the house symbol next to **room_menu**, this indicates that this will be the first room run when the game starts.

You can change the room order in Room Manager as shown in Figure C-34, by clicking and dragging to get the desired order.

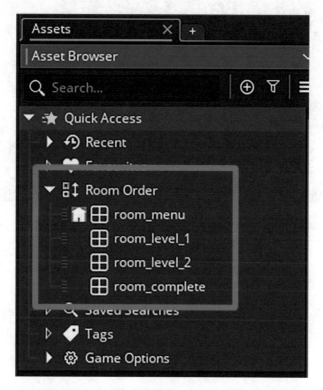

Figure C-34. *Showing how to change room order*

Paths

As mentioned previously, paths are preset patterns that can be used to make an instance move in a particular fashion. Paths can also be created dynamically through use of code. Figure C-35 shows an example of a path.

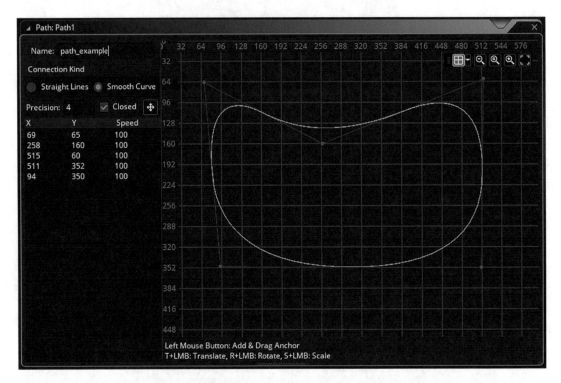

Figure C-35. *Showing an example of a path*

Functions

Functions are code snippets separate from the main code blocks in your game. Functions are great for

- Making code clearer and easier to update.

- When you have the same code in more than one place.

- Trying out some code separate from your main code.

Sequences

Sequences a way of making things move and happen in a predefined way. It can include images and audio. They can be used to great effect and can really simplify the process of making certain things happen.

Shaders

Shaders allow advanced image processing to make some seriously impressive things happen. This is not covered in this book in depth (it would take a whole book of its own just to cover the basics).If you fancy delving into this more, there are tons of great resources and examples online.

Tilesets

A great and quick method of designing backgrounds for your levels, using tiles requires less overhead than objects. There is a chapter dedicated to tile use.

Timelines

Timelines are awesome to make things happen at a preset time within your game. A great alternative to alarms. I like timelines especially for testing, as editing the timing can be done quickly with minimal fuss.

Target

Depending on the license you are subscribed to, different compile targets will be available, for example, as shown in Figure C-36.

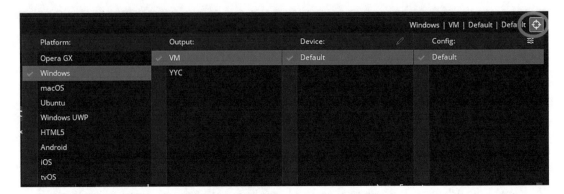

Figure C-36. *Showing available targets*

Note   If you recently made changes to your subscription package, you may need to quit and restart GameMaker before it shows up as available.

Naming Conventions

Keeping your project tidy and well-organized makes editing and tracking things a lot easier; I always use a naming convention, for example:

- For objects I use the prefix obj_

- For sprites I use the prefix spr_

- For audio I use the prefix snd_

- For backgrounds I use the prefix bg_

- For tilesets I use the prefix ts_

- And similar names for other assets

I also use descriptive names, so I can instantly tell what the actual asset is, for example:

- obj_splash_screen

- obj_hud

- snd_bullet_fire

- snd_explosion

- bg_space

Code blocks allow you to add a description; I suggest using this feature, for example:

```
/// @description Setup Variables
health=50;
x=room_width/2;
```

Index

© Ben Tyers 2023
B. Tyers, *GameMaker Fundamentals*, https://doi.org/10.1007/978-1-4842-8713-2

R

S

T, U

Printed in the United States
by Baker & Taylor Publisher Services